1999
FORMULA ONE
YEARBOOK

THE ESSENTIAL GUIDE TO
THE GRAND PRIX YEAR

A DORLING KINDERSLEY BOOK

FOREWORD

Welcome to the 1999 edition of the Formula One Yearbook. We have been treated to a season in which the fortunes of drivers and constructors have had more ups and downs than a trolley jack, making it a totally enthralling spectacle for every one of us who follows this aristocrat of motor sports.

In this year's edition we have made some minor changes in the way we have presented the information. We hope this will allow you to enjoy the book even more. Once again we have worked and schemed hard to get the book onto the streets within hours of the end of the season. Thanks go to the many people involved in this process. But the biggest thanks are saved for you, the reader, for playing the essential part in making the first edition so successful. We hope you like the 1999 edition and we look forward to making this annual publication proceed from strength to strength.

DORLING KINDERSLEY
LONDON • NEW YORK • NEW DELHI • SYDNEY

Publisher Mike Edwards
Senior managing art editor Derek Coombes
Production manager Sara Gordon

Produced for Dorling Kindersley by Grant Laing Partnership,
48 Brockwell Park Gardens, London SE24 9BJ

Editorial director Reg Grant
Design director Ruth Shane
Project editor Francis Ritter
Text Adrian Gilbert
Additional text Reg Grant
DTP Steve Wilson

CONTENTS

News from between the races appears after each grand prix.

Pre-Season Review

zepter
MasterCard
Heinz-Harald
FRENTZEN
PlayStation
BUZZIN HORNETS
BUZZIN HORNETS
HORNETS

Exit Goodyear and welcome to BAR

Formula One approached the 1999 season on the crest of a wave. Judging by worldwide television viewing figures, the sport was surpassed in popularity only by soccer World Cups and summer Olympics. Millions of fans eagerly awaited a re-run of the duel between the McLaren of Mika Hakkinen and Michael Schumacher's Ferrari that had ignited the previous season.

End of tyre wars

The biggest change for 1999 was the withdrawal of Goodyear from the Formula One scene. The "tyre wars" between Bridgestone, maker of the tyres used by McLaren, and Goodyear, manufacturer of the tyres preferred by Ferrari, had been at the heart of the previous year's contest. Now all the cars would be running on the same Bridgestone rubber.

New boys on the block

Another absentee for the new season would be the Tyrell team. Their place was taken by British American Racing (BAR), which immediately provoked the sharpest controversy of the pre-season. BAR planned to send out their two cars in different liveries, a move that brought swift disciplinary action from FIA bosses.

Efforts to arrange a Chinese Grand Prix failed, but Malaysia was added to the list of venues. European governmental pressure to end tobacco advertising in F1 seems set to hasten the search for new global venues.

Four-grooved Bridgestone tyres would be standard on all cars for 1999.

New season, new rules

The FIA, the governing body of Formula One racing, lays down strict regulations governing every aspect of car design. Major changes were introduced for the 1998 season, but this year has brought only relatively minor adjustments. These include:

• Four-grooved tyres. Last year, grooved tyres were made compulsory, a change intended to slow speeds in cornering and encourage overtaking. Front tyres had to have three grooves, and back tyres four. For the 1999 season, both back and front tyres must have four grooves.

• Fewer tyres per car. For this season, the number of dry-weather tyres allocated to each car for a grand prix weekend has been reduced from 40 to 32, as a result of the use of a harder rubber compound.

• Wheel cables. Cables will be attached to all wheels to prevent them becoming completely detached from the car in the event of a crash. Wheels flying loose have been identified as a major safety hazard, both for drivers and for race spectators.

• Panel lights. Drivers will now be able to receive information from track marshals through coloured lights on their dash panel.

McLaren: Racing to stay on top of the world

AFTER CARRYING OFF THE double prize of the constructors' and drivers' championships in 1998, McLaren-Mercedes could have been forgiven for resting on their laurels. But there was not the slightest trace of complacency in the team's approach to the new season.

Despite already having a car that had outperformed all the opposition, they worked tirelessly to develop a surprisingly different model for 1999, the MP4/14. Team chief Ron Dennis told journalists that fewer than 10 per cent of the parts on the car were carried over from the previous year.

Front runners

First reports of the new car suggested that McLaren would once again be the team to beat in 1999. The Mercedes engine is lighter and even more powerful than before. The only question-mark could be about the car's reliability.

In world champion Mika Hakkinen, McLaren have another trump card. The Finnish driver grew in stature through the 1998 season, proving cool under pressure as well as extremely fast. He is once more partnered by the Scottish driver David Coulthard.

Unlike their main rivals Ferrari, who insist that number two Eddie Irvine gives way to lead driver Michael Schumacher at all times, McLaren will let their two drivers compete. This suits Coulthard, who was disappointed to find himself playing second fiddle to Hakkinen last season. The Scot is keen to assert his own winning abilities. This may be a weakness for McLaren if the two drivers begin to take points off one another.

Keen and confident

Hakkinen looked confident and well rested when he met the press at the launch of the new car. Victory has not blunted his competitive edge. "I really want to win it again," he told journalists. And he clearly meant what he said.

Owner Ron Dennis has led McLaren to seven constructors' titles since 1984.

Designer Adrian Newey was a key figure in McLaren's 1998 success.

Team Profile

West-McLaren-Mercedes

Team Principal . . . . . . .Ron Dennis
Technical Director . . . .Adrian Newey

Address
McLaren International Ltd, Woking Business Park, Albert Drive, Woking, Surrey, GU21 5JY, UK

Internet
http://www.mclaren.co.uk

The Car

Chassis	McLaren MP4/14
Engine	Mercedes-Benz F0110H V10
Power	785 bhp
Tyres	Bridgestone
Fuel	Mobil

Results to end of 1998

GP Debut	GP Monaco 1966
GP Points	2203.5
GP Victories	116

Mika Hakkinen (car no. 1), born 28 September 1968 in Helsinki, Finland. F1 debut in the United States in 1991; to end of 1998, 112 starts, 9 wins.

David Coulthard (car no. 2), born 27 March 1971 in Twynholm, Scotland. F1 debut in Spain in 1994; to end of 1998, 74 starts, 4 wins.

The McLaren MP4/14 may prove an even more effective racing machine than last year's car.

Ferrari: Thirsting for a taste of glory

FERRARI ARE ACUTELY AWARE that it is 20 years since Jody Scheckter last won them the drivers' championship, and 16 years since they held the constructors' title. By most standards, the Italian team had an excellent season in 1998, ending as runners-up in both the drivers' and constructors' contest. But at Ferrari, that near-miss was regarded as a bitter failure.

For 1999, the Ferrari team presents an image of stability. Michael Schumacher remains number one driver, with Northern Ireland's Eddie Irvine in support. Jean Todt and technical supremo Ross Brawn are given another chance to mastermind the drive for honours. The car, however, has been quite thoroughly worked over, with a new chassis, a lighter, more powerful engine, and a lower centre of gravity. Goodyear's withdrawal from Formula One means that, this year, Ferrari will use Bridgestones.

The German question

If Schumacher again fails to top the drivers' table, some fans will claim that he was a great driver let down by his car. Yet critics point out that Schuey's aggression has led to mistakes that have ruined his own chances at crucial moments. Reportedly, the German is now a changed character, with a dash of sportsmanship and humility added to his steely character. If so, it can only improve his performance.

Irvine will once more be expected to play second fiddle, denied any chance of a win unless Schumacher goes out of the race.

Team Profile

Scuderia Ferrari Marlboro

Team Principal . . . . . . .Jean Todt
Technical Director . . . . .Ross Brawn

Address
Ferrari SpA, Via Ascari 55-57, 41053
Maranello, Modena, Italy

Internet
http://www.ferrari.it

The Car

Chassis . . . . .Ferrari F399
Engine . . . . .Ferrari 048 V10
Power . . . . .780 bhp
Tyres . . . . .Bridgestone
Fuel . . . . .Shell

Results to end of 1998

GP Debut . . . . . . GP Monaco 1950
GP Points 2226.5
GP Victories 119

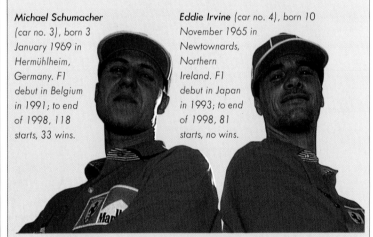

Michael Schumacher (car no. 3), born 3 January 1969 in Hermühlheim, Germany. F1 debut in Belgium in 1991; to end of 1998, 118 starts, 33 wins.

Eddie Irvine (car no. 4), born 10 November 1965 in Newtownards, Northern Ireland. F1 debut in Japan in 1993; to end of 1998, 81 starts, no wins.

Ferrari president
Luca di Montezemolo is haunted by his firm's glorious history, which sets formidably high expectations for the team's performance in the present day.

The F399 marks an evolutionary step forward from last season's F300.

Williams: Repairing the damage

IT IS IRONIC THAT SIR FRANK Williams was knighted by the Queen at the end of 1998, his most unsuccessful year of the decade. With not a single grand prix win to celebrate, the team that had carried off the constructors' title five times in the previous six years struggled to hold third place, almost 100 points adrift of Ferrari.

Predictable decline

This setback for Williams and his partner, technical director Patrick Head, was not entirely unexpected. They had lost their design wizard, Adrian Newey, to McLaren. And the withdrawal of Renault from Formula One had left Williams saddled with underpowered former Renault stock V10s – now serviced and supplied by Supertec – while waiting to make the transition to a BMW engine in the year 2000.

Not surprisingly, after such a chastening experience, it has been "all change" at Williams for 1999. A new car has been developed, the FW 21, described by Head as "quite adventurous". And out go former world champion Jacques Villeneuve

and Heinz-Harald Frentzen, replaced by Ralf Schumacher, moving across from Jordan, and Alessandro Zanardi, returning to Formula One from America.

Williams are gambling on the hunger of drivers with everything to prove. Ralf Schumacher has had to cope with being the brother of the more famous Michael, but his technical ability is outstanding. Aged 23, he must feel the time is right to begin to win.

American transfer

Zanardi performed disappointingly in Formula One in the early 1990s. The best result he achieved in 25 starts was sixth place for Lotus in the 1993 Brazilian Grand Prix. However, he enjoyed a complete change of fortune after making the decision to cross the Atlantic. He dominated IndyCar racing in 1997 and 1998, winning the CART world championship in both years. Whether he can now carry his American success back into grand prix racing is an open question.

Team Profile

Alessandro "Alex" Zanardi (car no. 5), born 23 October 1966 in Bologna, Italy. F1 debut in Spain in 1991; to end of 1998, 25 starts, no wins.

Winfield Williams F1

Team Principal . . .Sir Frank Williams
Technical Director Patrick Head

Address
Williams Grand Prix Engineering Ltd, Grove, Wantage, Oxon, OX12 0DQ, UK

Internet
http://www.williamsdb.force9.com

The Car

Chassis	. . . . .Williams FW21
Engine	. . . . .Supertec FB-01 V10
Power	. . . . .760 bhp
Tyres	. . . . .Bridgestone
Fuel	. . . . .Castrol

Results to end of 1998

GP Debut	. . . . . . .Argentina 1975
GP Points	. . . . . . .1948.5
GP Victories	103

Ralf Schumacher (car no. 6), born 30 June 1975 in Kerpen, Germany. F1 debut in Australia in 1997; to end of 1998, 33 starts, no wins.

Team leader Sir Frank Williams is used to success, with nine constructors' world titles to his name since 1980.

The FW21 is the first new Williams car since the departure of the team's designer, Adrian Newey, to rivals McLaren.

Jordan: Confident after first victory

Team Profile

Team leader Eddie Jordan.

Damon Hill (car no. 7), born 17 September 1960 in London, England. F1 debut in England in 1992; to end of 1998, 100 starts, 22 wins.

Heinz-Harald Frentzen (car no. 8), born 18 May 1967 in Mönchenglad-bach, Germany. F1 debut in Brazil in 1994; to end of 1998, 81 starts, 1 win.

Benson & Hedges Jordan-Mugen-Honda

Team Principal ....Eddie Jordan
Technical Director .Mike Gascoyne

Address
Jordan Grand Prix,
Silverstone, Towcester,
Northamptonshire, NN12 8JT, UK

Internet
http://www.jordangp.com

The Car

Chassis .Jordan 199
Engine . .Mugen-Honda MF301HD V10
Power . . .765 bhp
Tyres . . .Bridgestone
Fuel . . . . .Repsol

Results to end of 1998

GP Debut . . . . .GP USA 1991
GP Points 155
GP Victories 1

JORDAN EXPERIENCED A SEASON of two halves in 1998. The team began poorly, and after eight races had not scored a single point. But the second eight brought Jordan 34 points and placed them fourth in the constructors' championship, their best-ever ranking. The season also brought the team their first grand prix victory – after 127 starts. In the rain at Spa, Damon Hill seized the opportunity offered by a series of crashes that eliminated Ferrari and McLaren to steal first place, with team-mate Ralf Schumacher close behind.

Fancied outsiders

Largely on the strength of the team's storming end to the 1998 season, Jordan are widely fancied as the most likely outsiders to make a dent in the total dominance of McLaren and Ferrari in 1999.

Eddie Jordan's ambition is to make his team the leader of Formula One in the next decade. Capital is flowing in, both from sponsors Benson & Hedges and from an American investment group, Warburg Pincus, which has bought into Jordan's business.

This season, much will depend on how the ex-Tyrrell designer Mike Gascoyne shapes up, replacing Gary Anderson at the head of Jordan's technical team. Anderson had been with Jordan since the team began racing in Formula One in 1991, so this is a considerable leap in the dark.

Honda power

Certainly, the Mugen-Honda engine at Jordan's disposal is reliable and powerful – the extra horsepower from an improved version of the engine was one of the keys to the startling transformation of Jordan's fortunes last season.

Jordan's first victory at Spa was also Damon Hill's first win since 1996. The English driver had seemed on a downward path after his departure from Williams. But now, with a victory under his belt, his hunger may be sharpened.

This year Hill is paired with another Williams reject, Heinz-Harald Frentzen. The German driver will be desperately keen to show his true worth at Jordan after a bruising time with Williams.

With drivers of proven ability and a car that can challenge the best, Eddie Jordan's overwhelming enthusiasm for the sport may at last be rewarded with success.

Jordan believe they have a car that can press Ferrari and McLaren.

Benetton: In need of stability

Team Profile

Mild Seven Benetton Playlife

Team Principal . . .Rocco Benetton
Technical Director Pat Symonds

Address
Benetton Formula Ltd, Whiteways Technical Centre, Enstone, Chipping Norton, Oxon, OX7 4EE, UK

Internet
http://www.benetton.com/wwa/sport

The Car

Chassis . . . . .Benetton B199
Engine . . . . .Supertec FB 01
V10 (Playlife)
Power . . . . .760 bhp
Tyres . . . . .Bridgestone
Fuel . . . . .Agip

Results to end of 1998

GP Debut . . . . . . .GP Brazil 1986
GP Points 805.5
GP Victories 27

BEFORE THE LAST GRAND PRIX season, Benetton gambled on radical change to retrieve their failing fortunes. They had a new manager, Dave Richards, two new drivers, Giancarlo Fisichella and Alexander Wurz, and a new Mecachrome-Renault engine. Rather than settling down, however, the team soon underwent fresh mutations.

Back in the family

Dave Richards did not survive a season that ended with Benetton in fifth place in the constructors' championship. In the autumn, young Rocco Benetton took direct control of the Formula One team back into the family's hands.

Through the winter months, the team's design guru Nick Wirth developed a new car, the B199, that was brazenly trumpeted by Benetton as "revolutionary".

The car's most talked-of feature is a braking system known as Front Torque Transfer (FTT). This is supposed to distribute the load between the two front-wheel brakes to avoid lock-up. There were hints

that this might transform the chances of overtaking and hence give Benetton a competitive edge.

Preparing for the 1999 season, the team were bristling with optimism. Rocco Benetton told the press: "Our target is clear. We want to be back on top." The worst scenario he could envisage was that Benetton might end up "somewhere in the top three". Wirth talked of a "massive leap forward" in performance from the new car.

More detached observers noted that, despite being rechristened Playlife, the Benetton engine was still the Renault-Mecachrome that had proved inadequate in 1998.

Behind the wheel

Italian driver Fisichella and the tall Austrian Wurz have been retained, not carrying the can for Benetton's underperformance in their first year with the team. Fisichella will be especially hot for his first win, having scored two second places in 1998. Wurz failed to make it to the podium last year, but experts rate the Austrian's skills highly.

Described as a revolutionary new design, the Benetton B199 has excited high hopes for 1999.

Team principal Rocco Benetton, below, flanked by his drivers for 1999: Alexander Wurz (car no. 10), left, born 15 February 1974 in Waldhofen, Austria. F1 debut in Canada in 1997; to end of 1998, 19 starts, no wins. Giancarlo Fisichella (car no. 9), right, born 14 January 1973 in Rome, Italy. F1 debut in Australia in 1996; to end of 1998, 41 starts, no wins.

Sauber: Time for Swiss to start winning

THE SWISS TEAM SAUBER HAVE now been in the Formula One game for six years, without ever placing better than third in a grand prix. Team principal Peter Sauber knows that it is high time to begin making an impression on the points tables, if he wants to counter the scepticism of those who say the land of the cuckoo clock will never come up to scratch in Formula One.

Sauber's 1998 season was typified by the incident that put Johnny Herbert out of the Italian Grand Prix. A mechanic left a pair of pliers in his footwell, creating such problems for the driver that he eventually span off. It was hard to imagine such a lapse occurring in a leading Formula One team.

Positive points

Sauber finished with 10 points in the 1998 season. Yet there is no doubt that they have their positive side. The money that they receive from their sponsors, chiefly Petronas and Red Bull, has been augmented by a reputed £5 million of personal sponsorship brought in by their new driver for 1999, the Brazilian Pedro Diniz. A lot has been spent on developing the Ferrari-derived Petronas V10 engine. Above all, in Jean Alesi they have one of the most exciting drivers currently participating in Formula One.

Alesi is the most experienced driver on the circuit, with 151 grand prix starts by the end of 1998. The fact that he has one solitary grand prix victory to his name has damaged his reputation less than might have been expected. His

Team Profile

Pedro Diniz (car no. 12), above, born 22 May 1970 in Sao Paulo, Brazil. F1 debut in Brazil in 1995; to end of 1998, 66 starts, no wins.

Jean Alesi (car no. 11), above right, born 11 June 1964 in Avignon, France. F1 debut in France in 1989; to end of 1998, 151 starts, 1 win.

Team Principal Peter Sauber.

Red Bull Sauber Petronas

Team Principal . . . . . . .Peter Sauber
Technical Director . . . . .Leo Ress

Address
Red Bull Sauber Petronas, Wildbachstrasse 9, 8340 Hinwil, Switzerland

Internet
http://www.sauber.ch

The Car

Chassis . . . . .Sauber C18
Engine . . . . .Petronas Ferrari V10
Power . . . . .770 bhp
Tyres . . . . .Bridgestone
Fuel . . . . .Shell

Results to end of 1998

GP Debut . . . . .GP South Africa 1993
GP Points 79
GP Victories 0

flamboyant, cavalier style of driving has made him a major attraction to fans and insiders alike.

Well matched

Alesi's carefree manner has not prevented him from clocking up points with a high degree of consistency. But 1998 was a bad year for the French driver, with a third place in Belgium providing his only appearance on the podium. Sauber hope he will benefit from the departure of Johnny Herbert, who was replaced by Diniz. The gentlemanly Brazilian is not likely to contest Alesi's position as number one driver. If the pair prove well matched, they may at last allow Sauber to make their mark.

Sauber's powerful Ferrari-derived Petronas engine gives the Swiss-based team hope of success in 1999.

Arrows: Black Prince to the rescue

Team Profile

Arrows

Team Principals . . .Tom Walkinshaw
Malik Ado Ibrahim
Technical Director Mike Coughlan

Address
Arrows GP International, Leafield Technical
Centre, Leafield, Witney, Oxon, OX8 5PF, UK

Internet
http://www.arrows.com

The Car

Chassis . . . . . . .Arrows A20
Engine . . . . .Arrows Hart V10
Power . . . . .755 bhp
Tyres . . . . .Bridgestone
Fuel . . . . .Repsol

Results to end of 1998

GP Debut . . . . . .GP Brazil 1978
GP Points 156
GP Victories . . .0

Toranosuke Takagi (car no. 14), born 12 February 1974 in Shizuoka, Japan. F1 debut in Australia in 1998; to end of 1998, 16 starts, no wins.

Nigerian businessman Prince Malik Ado Ibrahim, above left, bought a controlling interest in Arrows in time for the start of the 1999 season.

Tom Walkinshaw took control of Arrows in 1996, but financial difficulties have blocked the path to success.

Pedro de la Rosa (car no. 15), born 24 February 1971 in Barcelona, Spain. Made his F1 debut in 1999.

WITHOUT A WIN IN 20 YEARS OF Formula One racing, Arrows are accustomed to simply making up the numbers at the rear of the field. Dramatic changes before the start of this year's season, however, have opened up the possibility of a fresh start for the Witney-based team.

Money matters

After another disappointing season in 1998, the team was facing severe financial problems. There was talk of a takeover by the German company Zakspeed or Japanese manufacturer Toyota. But in the end, the man who came forward with the money to salvage the Arrows team was Nigerian financier Prince Malik Ado Ibrahim.

Prince Malik raised £77 million to buy a 70 per cent interest in the company, leaving previous owner Tom Walkinshaw with 25 per cent. A businessman and car enthusiast, Malik stated his chief aim as expanding the appeal of Formula One beyond its European focus to a global audience. He told journalists: "There is no reason why the next Michael Schumacher can't be black."

Walkinshaw was left in charge of racing, while Malik took over the business side. The Arrows car would be built entirely in-house, including the engine, chassis, and gearbox. Malik promised a new design in the course of the season.

The driver set-up remained unsettled until just before the opening of the new season, when Finnish driver Mika Salo was dropped in favour of rookie Pedro de la Rosa, who will support Tora Takagi. The drivers' inexperience, with even Takagi yet to score a point, suggests that it will be some time before grandiose plans for the team's future come to fruition.

Stewart: Desperate for results

WHEN EX-WORLD CHAMPION driver Jackie Stewart announced he was starting a Formula One team in 1997, he said it would be five years before the new organization could become a serious competitor.

Even given this long-term perspective, however, the Stewart team's lack of progress in 1998 was disappointing. They notched up only five points, one less than in their debut year. No one could fault the professionalism of the Stewart outfit, but the car was plagued by mechanical failures, especially gearbox problems. All season, the team managed only 12 finishes.

Searching for solutions

The engine was refined in the course of 1998, searching for more power, but it was never seriously competitive. And Stewart never found a satisfactory second driver to back up the exciting talent of Brazilian Rubens Barrichello. They ditched Jan Magnussen in mid-season, only to find his replacement, Dutch driver Jos Verstappen, equally unsatisfactory.

For the 1999 season, there have been radical changes. Jackie Stewart has handed over day-to-day control of the team to his son, Paul. Top designer Gary Anderson has been brought in from Jordan. A promising new engine has appeared from Cosworth, now directly owned by

The SF-3 promises to be both more powerful and more reliable than the car Stewart fielded last year.

Ford. And Barrichello has been joined by an experienced partner, English driver Johnny Herbert.

Unfulfilled potential

Herbert had become discontented with his position at Sauber, where Jean Alesi was favoured at his expense. Between them, he and Barrichello have started in well over 200 grand prix, although both are drivers who have fallen short of fulfilling their potential. Hungry to make their mark after earlier disappointments, Herbert and Barrichello will be keen to ensure that this season real success at last comes their way.

This is regarded as a make-or-break year for Stewart. The former world champion may be prepared to take the long view, but engine-suppliers Ford are not so patient. They will expect to see results soon.

Team Profile

Father and son team: Jackie Stewart (right) and Paul Stewart listen in.

Johnny Herbert (car no. 17), born 27 June 1964 in Romford, Essex. F1 debut in Brazil in 1989; to end of 1998, 129 starts, 2 wins.

Stewart-Ford

Team Principals . . . . .Jackie Stewart
Paul Stewart
Technical Director . . .Gary Anderson
Address
Stewart Grand Prix, The Stewart Building, Bradbourne Drive, Tilbrook, Milton Keynes, Buckinghamshire, MK14 8BJ, UK
Internet
http://www.stew.

The Car

Chassis . . . . .Stewart-Ford SF-3
Engine . . . . .Ford Cosworth CR-1
Power . . . . .775 bhp
Tyres . . . . .Bridgestone
Fuel . . . . .Texaco

Results to end of 1998

GP Debut . . . . . . .GP Australia 1997
GP Points 11
GP Victories . .0

Rubens Barrichello (car no. 16), born 23 May 1972 in Sao Paulo, Brazil. F1 debut in South Africa in 1993; to end of 1998, 97 starts, no wins.

Prost hope that this year's car will give the drivers a better chance to compete.

Prost: Fighting for France

FRANCE HAS A PROUD HISTORY of success in motor sport and high-quality car design. The only French team currently in Formula One, Prost are under immense pressure to fulfil what has been, in recent years, a sadly frustrated national desire for grand prix victories.

The signs of high ambition at Prost are unmistakeable. Generously backed by Peugeot, owner Alain Prost has moved his headquarters to the outskirts of Paris and expanded the staff from 70 to around 200. He has also poached innovative designer John Barnard from Arrows.

And yet the dreadful season Prost endured in 1998 continues to cast a shadow over the team's future prospects. A sixth place in Belgium provided their solitary point-scoring performance of the year.

Lead driver Olivier Panis had an especially bad season. Part of the problem was the aftermath of the crash in the 1997 Canadian Grand Prix that broke both his legs. Panis drove throughout the 1998 season with a steel plate in each leg from the knee to the ankle. He was acutely aware of the risks he was taking, when even a slight accident might have ended his career.

Return to fitness

Panis has now declared himself 100 per cent fit after having the plates removed. "It was only minor surgery," he told journalists, "but it has lifted a dark cloud that was in my head all the way through 1998."

Prost's number two driver, Jarno Trulli, is widely considered one of the most promising young racers around. As an Italian, he suffers less from the pressure of the French aspirations that weigh so heavily on the shoulders of Prost and Panis.

In reality, the 1998 Prost-Peugeot car, which was both underpowered and difficult to handle, gave the drivers very little chance. In the new AP02, the team believe they have produced the vehicle that can put them right back on track.

Team Profile

Equipe Prost-Peugeot

Team Principal . . . . . Alain Prost
Technical Director . . John Barnard

Address
Prost Grand Prix, Quartier des Sangliers, 7 Avenue Eugene Freyssinet, 78280 Guyancourt, France

Internet
http://www.prost-peugeot.com

The Car

Chassis . . . . .Prost AP02
Engine . . . . .Peugeot A18 V10
Power . . . . .765 bhp
Tyres . . . . .Bridgestone
Fuel . . . . .Total

Results to end of 1998

GP Debut . . . . .GP Australia 1997
GP Points 22
GP Victories 0

Olivier Panis (car no. 18), born 2 September 1966 in Lyons, France. F1 debut in Brazil in 1994; to end of 1998, 81 starts, no wins.

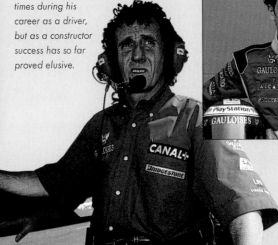

Alain Prost, below, topped the world championship four times during his career as a driver, but as a constructor success has so far proved elusive.

Jarno Trulli (car no. 19), born 13 July 1974 in Pescara, Italy. F1 debut in Australia in 1997; to end of 1998, 30 starts, no wins.

Minardi: An end to pointless run in sight?

FOR THE LAST THREE SEASONS, Minardi have failed to score a single championship point. The Italian minnows have earned a certain affection and respect for their enthusiastic perseverance in the face of repeated failures. But there are signs that the team is beginning to tire of life at the back of the grid and aspire to higher achievement.

Fresh talent

The team is increasingly dominated by Italian industrialist Gabriele Rumi, who has a more aggressive approach than team founder and co-owner Giancarlo Minardi. Rumi poached top designer Gustav Brunner from Ferrari in 1998, and the fruit of Brunner's labours is unveiled this year – the Minardi M01. Powered by a Ford works engine, the new car just might give Minardi a chance to compete.

Another newcomer to Minardi is experienced sporting manager Cesare Fiorio. He will have his work cut out to get the best from his drivers, rookie Marc Gené and Ferrari test driver Luca Badoer.

Spanish money

Minardi had intended to persist with the young Argentinian driver Esteban Tuero who joined them in 1998, but Tuero apparently decided that grand prix racing was not for him. To fill the gap, in came Spanish driver Gené. His lack of experience or obvious qualification for the job was overlooked in the light of the substantial sponsorship he brought with him from Telefonica, the Spanish communications giant.

Badoer, by contrast, is a driver with an established reputation. He first drove in Formula One in 1993, after wining the F3000 trophy the previous year. Although his racing career failed to take off, his work as test driver for Ferrari since 1998 has been highly praised. He will stay in his Ferrari role while racing for Minardi, who must hope they are not treated as a sideline.

The introduction of the Minardi M01 is intended to mark the start of a new era for the team from Faenza.

Team Profile

Team founder Giancarlo Minardi.

Marc Gené (car no. 21), above left, born 29 March 1974 in Sabadell, Spain. F1 debut in 1999.

Luca Badoer (car no. 20), above right, born 25 January 1971 in Montebelluna, Italy. F1 debut in South Africa in 1993; to end of 1998, 34 starts, no wins.

Fondmetal Minardi Ford

Team Principals . . .Gabriele Rumi
Giancarlo Minardi
Technical Director . .Gustav Brunner
Address
Minardi Team SpA, Via Spallanzani 21, 48018 Faenza, Italy
Internet
http://www.minardi.it

The Car

Chassis . . . . .Minardi M01
Engine . . . . .Ford Zetec-R V10
Power . . . . .775 bhp
Tyres . . . . .Bridgestone
Fuel . . . . .Minardi

Results to end of 1998

GP Debut . . . . . .GP Brazil 1985
GP Points 27
GP Victories 0

BAR: The new team starts with a zip

BRITISH AMERICAN RACING (BAR) made their entrance into Formula One before the 1998 season by buying the Tyrrell team. However, this is the first season that BAR will race under their own name.

A winning hand

On paper, the new outfit has a string of trumps in its hand. British American Tobacco has stumped up plenty of cash to fund the team. Craig Pollock, the mastermind behind BAR, is a man of undoubted intelligence and ability. The immensely experienced constructor Adrian Reynard has come on board to provide the car. And Pollock has brought in former world champion Jacques Villeneuve as lead driver, supported by Ricardo Zonta.

The close relationship between Pollock and Villeneuve is at the heart of the concept of the BAR team. Pollock has been the Canadian driver's racing mentor and manager, and clearly sees BAR as a vehicle to launch him to a second world championship.

Livery controversy

Famous for his frequent changes of hair colour, Villeneuve is one of grand prix racing's great non-conformists. The BAR team seemed to bear the same stamp when it unconventionally planned to race its cars in two different liveries. The FIA quashed this idea, but the "zipped" combination of the two liveries adopted by BAR still smacks of cheek.

There is no doubt that, possessing the right finance, personnel, and technical setup, the team is capable of scoring points in its debut year. Pollock is confident, but aware of the possible gap between promise and performance. "It's on the track where BAR must make their mark," he told the press. "I believe we're capable of doing just that."

Team Profile

Managing Director Craig Pollock flanked by drivers Jacques Villeneuve (left) and Ricardo Zonta. Villeneuve (car no. 22), born 9 April 1971 in St Jean-sur-Richelieu, Canada. F1 debut in Australia in 1996; to end of 1998, 49 starts, 11 wins. Zonta (car no. 23), born 23 March 1976 in Curitiba, Brazil. Made his F1 debut in 1999.

BAR-Supertec

Team Principal . . . . .Craig Pollock
Technical Director . .Adrian Reynard

Address
British American Racing, Brackley, Northamptonshire, NN13 7BD, UK

Internet
http://www.britishamericanracing.com

The Car

Chassis . . . . . . .BAR 001
Engine . . . . . . .Supertec FB01 V10
Power . . . . . . .760 bhp
Tyres . . . . . . .Bridgestone
Fuel . . . . .Elf

Results to end of 1998

GP Debut . . . . .GP Australia 1999
GP Points . . . . .not applicable
GP Victories . .not applicable

The BAR car shows off its dual livery of Lucky Strike and State Express 555, joined in the middle by a giant zip. The chassis was produced by Adrian Reynard.

The 1999 Season

The Race Diary

Australian Grand Prix, Melbourne, 7 March

Brazilian Grand Prix, São Paulo, 11 April

San Marino Grand Prix, Imola, 2 May

Monaco Grand Prix, Monte Carlo, 16 May

Spanish Grand Prix, Barcelona, 30 May

Canadian Grand Prix, Montreal, 13 June

French Grand Prix, Magny-Cours, 27 June

British Grand Prix, Silverstone, 11 July

Austrian Grand Prix, A1-Ring, 25 July

German Grand Prix, Hockenheim, 1 August

Hungarian Grand Prix, Hungaroring, 15 August

Belgian Grand Prix, Spa-Francorchamps, 29 August

Italian Grand Prix, Monza, 12 September

European Grand Prix, Nürburgring, 26 September

Malaysian Grand Prix, Sepang, 17 October

Japanese Grand Prix, Suzuka, 31 October

Australian Grand Prix

"The race is not to the swift," says the Bible, and this was certainly the story of the opening grand prix of the season. Although the Mercedes-powered McLarens of Mika Hakkinen and David Coulthard proved themselves by far the fastest cars in qualifying and led from the start in the race itself, they failed to finish. With Michael Schumacher's afternoon also ruined by mechanical failures, it was Ferrari number two, Eddie Irvine, who took the chequered flag — recording his first grand prix victory at the 82nd attempt. Irvine's unexpected win suggested that a less predictable season than last year might be in prospect.

Eddie Irvine celebrates his first grand prix victory in traditional style.

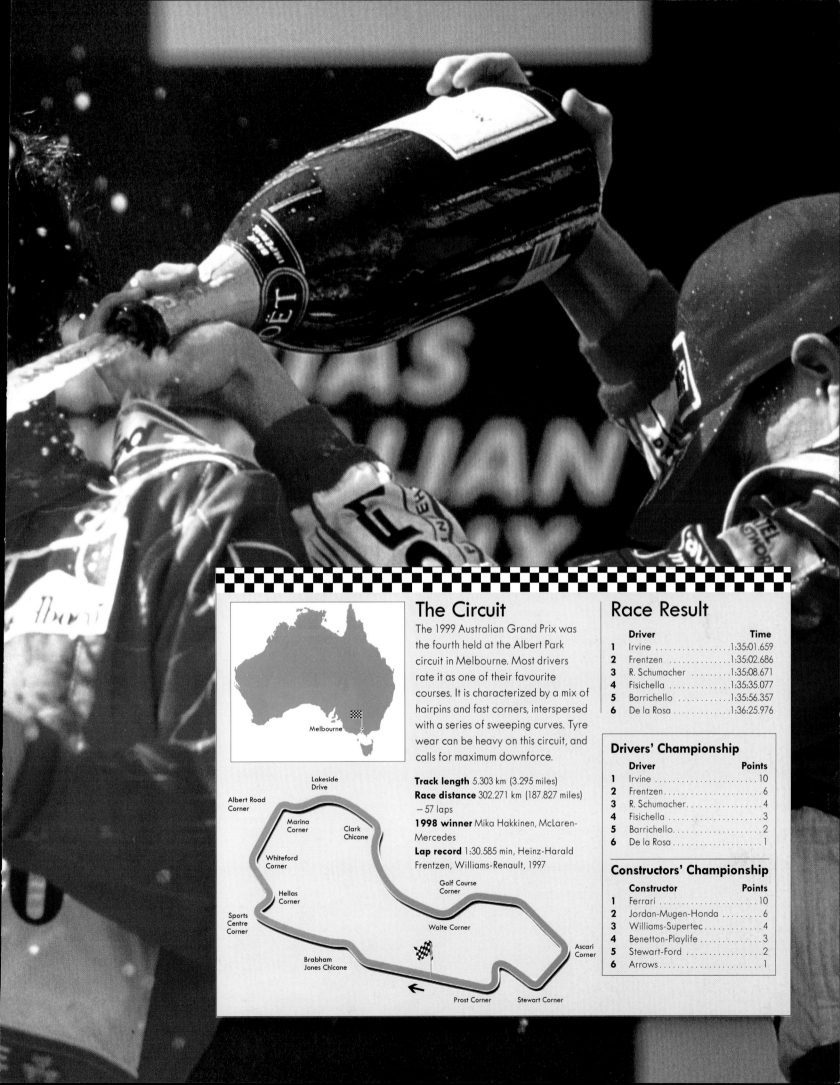

The Circuit

The 1999 Australian Grand Prix was the fourth held at the Albert Park circuit in Melbourne. Most drivers rate it as one of their favourite courses. It is characterized by a mix of hairpins and fast corners, interspersed with a series of sweeping curves. Tyre wear can be heavy on this circuit, and calls for maximum downforce.

Track length 5.303 km (3.295 miles)
Race distance 302.271 km (187.827 miles) — 57 laps
1998 winner Mika Hakkinen, McLaren-Mercedes
Lap record 1:30.585 min, Heinz-Harald Frentzen, Williams-Renault, 1997

Melbourne

Lakeside Drive
Albert Road Corner
Marina Corner
Clark Chicane
Whiteford Corner
Hellas Corner
Sports Centre Corner
Brabham Jones Chicane
Prost Corner
Stewart Corner
Waite Corner
Golf Course Corner
Ascari Corner

Race Result

	Driver	Time
1	Irvine	1:35:01.659
2	Frentzen	1:35:02.686
3	R. Schumacher	1:35:08.671
4	Fisichella	1:35:35.077
5	Barrichello	1:35:56.357
6	De la Rosa	1:36:25.976

Drivers' Championship

	Driver	Points
1	Irvine	10
2	Frentzen	6
3	R. Schumacher	4
4	Fisichella	3
5	Barrichello	2
6	De la Rosa	1

Constructors' Championship

	Constructor	Points
1	Ferrari	10
2	Jordan-Mugen-Honda	6
3	Williams-Supertec	4
4	Benetton-Playlife	3
5	Stewart-Ford	2
6	Arrows	1

Stars are eclipsed by lesser lights

Damon Hill shows his frustration at going out on the first lap.

Qualification

McLaren's performance in the first qualifying session of the year delivered a severe shock to the competition, especially Ferrari. Mika Hakkinen and David Coulthard occupied the front of the grid with ease, showing that once again the McLaren-Mercedes had the quickest, most powerful cars on the track by a long stretch. Behind the McLaren pair, Ferrari's white hope Michael Schumacher performed heroics to hoist an unsatisfactory-looking car up to third place.

Hakkinen knows he is the fastest.

Stewart looked impressive, with Rubens Barrichello making fourth, and for Jordan Heinz-Harald Frentzen easily outstripped team-mate Damon Hill to line up on the third rank alongside the Ferrari number two, Eddie Irvine.

Qualifying Times

1	Hakkinen	McLaren-Mercedes	1:30.462
2	Coulthard	McLaren-Mercedes	1:30.946
3	M. Schumacher	Ferrari	1:31.781
4	Barrichello	Stewart-Ford	1:32.148
5	Frentzen	Jordan-Mugen-Honda	1:32.276
6	Irvine	Ferrari	1:32.289
7	Fisichella	Benetton-Playlife	1:32.540
8	R. Schumacher	Williams-Supertec	1:32.691
9	Hill	Jordan-Mugen-Honda	1:32.695
10	Wurz	Benetton-Playlife	1:32.789
11	Villeneuve	BAR-Supertec	1:32.888
12	Trulli	Prost-Peugeot	1:32.971
13	Herbert	Stewart-Ford	1:32.991
14	Diniz	Sauber-Petronas	1:33.374
15	Zanardi	Williams-Supertec	1:33.549
16	Alesi	Sauber-Petronas	1:33.910
17	Takagi	Arrows	1:34.182
18	De la Rosa	Arrows	1:34.244
19	Zonta	BAR-Supertec	1:34.412
20	Panis	Prost-Peugeot	1:35.068
21	Badoer	Minardi-Ford	1:35.316
Gené (Minardi) was outside the qualifying time.			

This was a race to give hope to all understudies and rookies. Not only did Irvine slip the leash that ties him to Schumacher's service, but De la Rosa came sixth in his first grand prix – on an occasion when two former world champions, Villeneuve and Hill, and reigning champion Hakkinen failed to stay the course. Will there ever be another grand prix in which the two Arrows cars finish ahead of Schumacher?

The race began in chaotic fashion as the Stewart team started the season in a blaze – but not of glory. Both of their cars caught fire on the grid, forcing a restart. Barrichello got the Stewart spare car, while his English team-mate Herbert, confirming his reputation as an unlucky driver, was left to sit the race out.

Sent to the back

Schumacher also got off to a bad start. He could not find first gear as the cars drew away for a second formation lap, and was relegated to the back row of the grid for the restart. So Irvine found himself leading the Ferrari effort.

The McLarens immediately set the pace, as expected, streaking away from the field, with Mika Hakkinen holding the edge over Coulthard. By lap 13, Irvine was 17 seconds down on the two leaders, without a hope of getting in touch. The race looked set to be a repeat of the opening to the 1998 season, when McLaren scored a one-two walkover.

McLaren breakdown

But soon everything began to fall apart for the Silver Arrows, as the vaunted new MP4/14s revealed a fatal lack of reliability. First, Coulthard limped into the pits, with his gears jammed due to a problem with the hydraulics. As he said later, it was a case of "game over, park it, and get a suntan".

Next came the Finnish driver's turn to suffer. He was out in front on his own when the safety car was

introduced on lap 13, a consequence of Jacques Villeneuve crashing out. All the cars bunched up behind the Finn. When racing resumed, Hakkinen could not regain speed. The suddenly dawdling leader caused havoc behind him, as cars tried to avoid overtaking before the start-finish line – and thus receiving a stop-go penalty – but also to avoid running into one another.

When the chaos cleared away, Irvine and Frentzen found themselves out in front. Hakkinen limped on with a defective throttle until lap 21 before pulling out of the race.

Alex will have to mind the gap

Alessandro "Alex" Zanardi arrived at Williams this year fresh from a string of triumphs in American Champ Car racing. However, his experience at Melbourne will have reminded him of the yawning gap between Formula One and the North American circuit.

Zanardi could only qualify 15th on the grid. In the race itself, he was lapping three seconds slower than his team-mate, Ralf Schumacher, when he smashed into the wall. His comment on the crash was: "I don't know what happened." It probably expressed his feeling about the whole experience of the race.

Alex Zanardi enjoys the glamour of Formula One racing Down Under.

Right: Irvine forges on, with Frentzen in pursuit. The German gave Jordan their best ever start to a season.

Michael Schumacher was driving very fast and might still have mounted a challenge from the back, but luck was against him. He had to pit with a puncture on lap 27, and later had to switch steering wheels. This left the German with no higher ambition than to stay the course.

Schumacher's misfortune was Irvine's opportunity. The Ferrari number two clearly revelled in the chance to abandon his habitual supporting role and go full out for victory. Only Frentzen might have caught him, but problems with the throttle on his Jordan left him unable to mount a serious challenge.

Rising talent

Frentzen's performance was one of the revelations of the grand prix. Eddie Jordan celebrated his team's best ever start to the championship, praising his new driver as "a great talent". In sad contrast, Frentzen's team-mate Damon Hill, driving in his 100th grand prix, failed to complete the first lap, finishing up in the gravel trap on the second corner.

Despite their trouble on the starting grid, Stewart were almost as pleased with their performance as Jordan. Barrichello believed that he would have had a serious chance of winning, but for a stop-go penalty and an unscheduled pit-stop.

Finally, though, the day belonged to Irvine. McLaren sportingly made him a gift of the champagne they had kept on ice to celebrate their own expected victory. They may have felt they had already gifted him the race.

As the stars stumbled, Arrows newcomer Pedro de la Rosa, right, nipped in to take a creditable sixth place.

BETWEEN THE RACES

8 March *Unimpressed by Irvine victory*

Talking to the press after the grand prix, everyone seemed determined to minimize the importance of the result at Melbourne. Despite Eddie Irvine's win, Ferrari team manager Jean Todt was clear that there would be no change in the strategy that forces the Northern Ireland driver to give way to Michael Schumacher at all times. "This was a very good result for Eddie," Todt said, "but tomorrow is another day."

Meanwhile, in the McLaren camp, confidence seemed to be undented by the failure of either driver to finish. Team Principal Ron Dennis declared himself "encouraged" by the new car's performance, while driver David Coulthard suggested that Irvine would be incapable of sustaining "a season-long challenge" for the championship.

8 March *Driver in the money*

The American business publication Forbes Magazine has placed Michael Schumacher at number 35 in its list of the 50 highest-paid celebrities in the world. The magazine estimates the German driver's income at $38 million a year. Schuey ranks just above movie heart-throb Leonardo DiCaprio.

Motor sport still cannot match basketball as a source of star earnings, however. The highest-paid sports celebrity is Michael Jordan, earning a cool $69 million a year. Schumacher has the consolation of being the world's second-richest sportsman.

BAR's plan to race a car in Lucky Strike livery alongside this one was vetoed by the FIA.

12 March *BAR ducks punishment in livery dispute*

BAR have escaped punishment from the FIA in the dispute over livery that has livened up their first season in Formula One. The BAR management had been called upon to answer charges of bringing the sport into disrepute, and faced the possibility of a heavy fine or even a racing ban.

The dispute exploded in the pre-season, when BAR unveiled their plan to put out their two cars in different liveries, one advertising Lucky Strike and the other State Express 555. The dual livery was apparently part of the deal struck between BAR and its main sponsors, tobacco giant BAT.

Formula One bosses responded angrily to the two-livery plan. Max Mosley reportedly said that it was "as if BAR were sticking two fingers up at the FIA and the whole Formula One establishment". When the FIA ordered the team to race their two cars in the same livery, BAR's lawyers lodged a complaint with the European Union, claiming that the FIA's action breached laws on free competition.

It was this bold legal challenge to the FIA that led to the charge of bringing the sport into disrepute. Called to appear in front of the FIA Council, BAR managing director Craig Pollock was forced to disown the legal action, claiming that lawyers had acted without his knowledge. Pollock made a full apology and promised to respect the FIA's authority. In return, the FIA chose to be lenient, although it reiterated the need for teams such as BAR to find alternatives to tobacco sponsorship in the near future.

22 March *Schumacher junior*

Michael Schumacher and his wife Corinna have had a baby boy. It is their second child. Schumacher reportedly suffered from nerves during testing at Jerez because of the imminent birth.

22 March *McRae for F1?*

According to the British press, 1995 world rally champion Colin McRae is to be given a chance to break into Formula One. Driving for Ford, McRae is currently in the lead in the Rally of Portugal. A Ford spokesman said that McRae would be given a test at the wheel of a Formula One car some time later in the year.

Eddie Irvine, right, and David Coulthard both itch to shake off the role of second fiddle.

8 April *Irvine aims to lead*

Winning in Australia has whetted Eddie Irvine's appetite for a less subservient role at Ferrari. Although he told the press that he could not argue with the Ferrari bosses' belief that Michael Schumacher was their best hope of winning the drivers' championship, he also commented: "If I win on a few occasions and Michael has a few problems, then maybe the situation with the team might change."

Irvine's contract obliges him to give way if Schumacher has a chance of winning, although, as Irvine is generally the slower of the two, this occurs only infrequently. By contrast, at McLaren, Mika Hakkinen and David Coulthard are allowed to compete. McLaren boss Ron Dennis says: "Mika and David can race each other, but they are instructed not to take each other off."

Michael Schumacher, currently the second highest-paid sports celebrity in the world, thanks to Ferrari.

Pit-stops – where races are lost and won

A PIT-STOP OFFERS AN AMAZING spectacle of perfectly co-ordinated movement under intense pressure. At least 17 mechanics are required to carry out a stop: two to operate the front and rear quick-lift jacks; four sub-teams of three to remove and replace each wheel; two to carry out the refuelling; and lastly the chief mechanic, who controls the operation by holding the stop board (which is also known as the lollipop).

Perfect braking

Other team members on hand in the pits include a refuelling assistant, an engine technician, and two more mechanics to wipe the driver's visor and check for debris around the air intakes. The driver also has a vital part to play in the operation. He must brake perfectly to bring his car to a stop at the right spot. If he errs by more than a few inches either way, precious seconds can be lost.

Fuelling hazard

The first pit-stop took place in 1957, but it was not until the early 1980s that pitting became a regular part of the Formula One scene. From 1983 until 1994, the pit-stop consisted of tyre changes, since refuelling was banned for safety reasons – a single drop of fuel on the exhaust can produce an instantaneous fire. This has only happened once, however, when Jos Verstappen's Benetton was transformed into a fireball in the first season after the practice of refuelling

Pit crews perform their vital task: the Ferrari team, right, and Jordan-Mugen-Honda, below.

was reintroduced. Thanks to their protective overalls, the driver and pit crew received only minor burns.

Winning strategies

Deciding how many pit-stops to take and when is, of course, crucial. Ferrari are the masters of pitting at the right moment. In a typical scenario,

technical director Ross Brawn will keep Michael Schumacher out a little longer than his rivals. Once they have gone in, Schumacher puts in a series of blistering laps on a low fuel load, gaining a few seconds before he races into the pits for his stop. He then emerges on to the track just ahead of his bemused rivals.

Brazilian Grand Prix

The romance of this year's grand prix at Interlagos lasted for 24 laps, the period when local hero Rubens Barrichello led the race at the wheel of his Stewart. The Brazilian driver's fine performance roused the crowd of 120,000 to unbridled excitement, before a pit-stop lost him the lead and, finally, mechanical failure ended his race. Reality reasserted itself in the shape of another straight contest between Mika Hakkinen and Michael Schumacher. The Finn needed all his famed coolness under pressure to cope with a sudden gear failure on the third lap that might have ruined his day. In the end, a faster car and superior tactics brought him victory over his German rival. Behind the leaders, Heinz-Harald Frentzen and Ralf Schumacher again performed well, while Eddie Irvine did just enough to stay at the top of the drivers' championship.

Rubens Barrichello proves that the Stewart-Ford can compete with McLaren and Ferrari — at least for half of a race.

The Circuit

São Paulo

The Interlagos circuit is situated on the southern outskirts of São Paulo. It is officially called the Autodromo José Carlos Pace, after the winner of the 1975 Brazilian Grand Prix. The track is bumpy and tiring for the drivers. The best opportunity for overtaking is presented by the chicane at the end of the start-finish straight, the "S" do Senna. The overall mix of slow and fast curves tests both cars and drivers.

Track length 4.292 km (2.667 miles)
Race distance 309.024 km (192.024 miles) — 72 laps
1998 winner Mika Hakkinen, McLaren-Mercedes
Lap record 1:18.397 min, Jacques Villeneuve, Williams-Renault, 1997

Bico de Pato
Mergulho
Pinheirinho
Ferradura
Junção
"S" do Senna
Curva do Sol
Descida do Lago
Reta Oposta

Race Result

	Driver	Time
1	Hakkinen	1:38:03.765
2	M. Schumacher	1:38:08.710
3	Frentzen	1 lap behind
4	R. Schumacher	1 lap behind
5	Irvine	1 lap behind
6	Panis	1 lap behind

Drivers' Championship

	Driver	Points
1	Irvine	12
2	Hakkinen	10
	=Frentzen	10
4	R. Schumacher	7
5	M. Schumacher	6
6	Fisichella	3
7	Barrichello	2
8	De la Rosa	1
	=Panis	1

Constructors' Championship

	Constructor	Points
1	Ferrari	18
2	McLaren-Mercedes	10
	=Jordan-Mugen Honda	10
4	Williams-Supertec	7
5	Benetton-Playlife	3
6	Stewart-Ford	2
7	Arrows	1
	=Prost-Peugeot	1

Mika's message is: "Business as usual"

Qualification

The grand prix Saturday began in dramatic fashion. BAR's Brazilian driver Ricardo Zonta had to be flown to hospital after a massive accident during free practice. The day got no better for BAR in qualifying, as Jacques Villeneuve was relegated to the back of the grid after stewards discovered evidence of a "fuel irregularity".

Silver Arrows on target

As at Melbourne, qualifying presented McLaren-Mercedes with a chance to demonstrate their clear superiority in speed. Hakkinen and Coulthard took the front row of the grid with ease.

Michael Schumacher reaffirmed his position as Ferrari number one by qualifying ahead of Irvine. But he failed to occupy the third place on the grid, pipped by the Stewart of Barrichello, a driver inspired by the dream of winning a grand prix in his home country.

Best of the rest

With Stewart performing impressively, the battle to be "best of the rest" behind McLaren and Ferrari was hotting up. Fisichella kept up Benetton's pretentions, qualifying fifth. Jordan occupied the fourth row, with Hill edging ahead of Frentzen. The Williams drivers, by contrast, had a poor session, qualifying 11th and 17th.

Qualifying Times

1	Hakkinen	McLaren-Mercedes	1:16.568
2	Coulthard	McLaren-Mercedes	1:16.715
3	Barrichello	Stewart-Ford	1:17.305
4	M. Schumacher	Ferrari	1:17.578
5	Fisichella	Benetton	1:17.810
6	Irvine	Ferrari	1:17.843
7	Hill	Jordan-Mugen-Honda	1:17.884
8	Frentzen	Jordan-Mugen-Honda	1:17.902
9	Wurz	Benetton	1:18.334
10	Herbert	Stewart-Ford	1:18.374
11	R. Schumacher	Williams-Supertec	1:18.506
12	Panis	Prost-Peugeot	1:18.636
13	Trulli	Prost-Peugeot	1:18.684
14	Alesi	Sauber	1:18.716
15	Diniz	Sauber	1:19.194
16	Villeneuve	BAR-Supertec	1:19.337*
17	Zanardi	Williams-Supertec	1:19.542
18	De la Rosa	Arrows	1:19.979
19	Sarrazin	Minardi-Ford	1:20.016
20	Takagi	Arrows	1:20.096
21	Gené	Minardi-Ford	1:20.710
* Villeneuve's time was disallowed.			

After the upsets of the opening grand prix at Melbourne, it was a return to "business as usual" at Interlagos. Hakkinen and Schumacher resumed their duel of last season, and once again the Finn looked as if he would have the edge. Only Frentzen was not lapped by the front two, and he failed to reach the finish line, running out of fuel late enough still to be classed third.

McLaren-Mercedes were only too aware that, in the previous grand prix, they had fallen prey to technical gremlins after totally dominating in the qualifying session. The start at Interlagos suggested that more frustration might be in store, as Coulthard stalled on the grid, only

Hakkinen signals another victory, despite worrying problems with his gears.

Frentzen's Jordan, right, did not quite make it to the finish, but he was still placed third.

narrowly avoiding being hit by Schumacher. The Scottish driver was eventually able to join the race from the pit lane, but he was three laps down, and more car trouble finally forced him to retire on lap 27.

Out of gear

Soon after the start, Hakkinen was also in trouble. On lap 3, he was surging ahead, putting a growing distance between himself and Barrichello in pursuit, when his gearbox stuck. Describing the incident later, Hakkinen said: "I selected a higher gear, but instead of it going through, there was no gear at all. I thought it was all over for me, but the team told me to continue, and the gears came back."

By the time Hakkinen had his gear

Give me a lift: Coulthard retired from the race on lap 27.

problem under control, he was in third place, with Barrichello and Schumacher ahead of him.

The Brazilian was enjoying the drive of his life, urged on by the enthusiasm of the crowd. But he faced a pit-stop problem, as Stewart had chosen to use softer-compound Bridgestones, rather than the harder compound selected by McLaren and Ferrari. This meant two stops for Barrichello, against only one for Hakkinen and Schuey.

Losing the lead

The Brazilian driver pitted on lap 27 and rejoined the race in fourth position. After that, he never looked a likely winner. On lap 44 his Ford engine gave up in a cloud of smoke. To the audible disappointment of the

vocally partisan São Paulo crowd, Barrichello's race was over.

Meanwhile, a sackful of other incidents had come and gone in the leaders' wake. Damon Hill had another disastrous afternoon. His team-mate Frentzen was behind him on the grid but surged ahead at the start to once more lead the Jordan charge. Driving rashly to recover ground, Hill collided with Wurz on lap 10 and was forced to retire.

Crashing out

French driver Stéphane Sarrazin, a late substitute for Minardi's injured Luca Badoer, went out in more spectacular fashion, crashing into the wall at around 290 km/h (180 mph). Luckily, he emerged unhurt.

Sarrazin's compatriot Jean Alesi also attracted attention, tearing through the field from the rear of the grid and, at one point, proving the fastest man on the circuit. Alesi disappointingly retired on lap 30.

Two-horse race

Hakkinen and Schumacher were finally left to fight it out between them. The Finn bided his time, waiting for Schumacher's pit-stop to take over the lead. He then turned up the heat, putting in a sequence of searing laps before pitting himself on lap 43. He was able to rejoin still in the lead, and the race was as good as under his belt. Schumacher kept up the pressure as best he could, but Hakkinen cruised comfortably home without really going flat out.

Hakkinen's McLaren leads from Barrichello's Stewart on the first lap, with Michael Schumacher in hot pursuit.

Schumacher's pit-stop cost him the lead and, ultimately, the race.

BETWEEN THE RACES

14 April *Death of "the Doc" saddens Formula One*

Harvey Postlethwaite, an influential figure in the world of Formula One since the 1970s, has died at the age of 55. He suffered a fatal heart attack while supervising testing of his latest car, intended to spearhead the return of Japanese manufacturer Honda to grand prix racing.

Postlethwaite entered Formula One in 1971 on the strength of a PhD in mechanical engineering – this was the qualification that earned him his nickname, "the Doc". After a short spell with March, Postlethwaite joined the unconventional Hesketh team, where he masterminded the car that enabled James Hunt to score his first grand prix victory. Moving on to work for Austrian magnate Walter Wolf, he created the Wolf WR1-4, a car which gave Jody Scheckter three wins in 1977.

In 1981, Postlethwaite was headhunted by Ferrari. He coped surprisingly well with the highly charged atmosphere at Maranello, confirming his reputation as an innovative designer by inspiring the Scuderia to the constructors' title in 1982 and 1983. He learned to speak fluent Italian and began collecting classic Ferraris as a hobby.

By the end of the decade, however, Postlethwaite was back in Britain to work with Ken Tyrrell. Apart from one brief and frustrating return to Ferrari, he stayed at Tyrrell until the team was bought out by BAR in 1998.

This would have seemed a very reasonable moment for "the Doc" to

The Honda test car that was preparing for the Japanese firm's return to F1.

Harvey Postlethwaite, English technical wizard, lays down the law during his successful spell at Ferrari.

retire, but the fascination of Formula One was too great for a man who had devoted the best part of his life to the sport. He became involved in Honda's plans to re-enter Formula One as a constructor as well as an engine supplier. Many Tyrrell stalwarts found themselves re-employed in work on a test chassis that was soon looking threateningly fast.

Jordan's technical director, Mike Gascoyne, who learned his trade working for Postlethwaite at Tyrrell, said: "His infectious enthusiasm for everything about Formula One was an inspiration." He will be remembered with respect and affection.

26 April *Salo on as substitute*

Finnish driver Mika Salo has been signed by BAR to replace the injured Ricardo Zonta in the San Marino Grand Prix. A Formula One driver since 1994, Salo is widely regarded as a driver of great talent who has

been hampered by the lack of a good car, first at Tyrrell and then at Arrows. He has been out of racing this season after failing to renew his contract with the Arrows team.

28 April: *Honda link with BAR*

Unconfirmed rumours suggest that Honda have agreed to supply engines to Craig Pollock's BAR team in the year 2000. The death of Honda's development director, Harvey Postlethwaite, seems to have decided the Japanese firm against entering their own team in Formula One as earlier planned.

If the rumours are true, the move will be seen as fresh evidence of the increasing takeover of Formula One teams by manufacturers. German car giant BMW will be supplying Williams with engines in 2000 and will no doubt expect to have a major influence on the team, as Mercedes do at McLaren. Ford are also becoming more pro-active in their relationship with Stewart.

29 April *Ferrari "too slow" says Irvine*

In the run-up to the San Marino Grand Prix, Ferrari driver Eddie Irvine has told the press that the team's cars are simply not quick enough to beat the McLarens, with their Mercedes-Benz engines. "I know I'm not able to go faster than the McLarens," Irvine said, "and it leaves me feeling cheesed off."

Irvine's statement may seem the plainest truth to followers of Formula One, but it is unlikely to please his Ferrari bosses. Rumours are rife that, come what may, this will probably be "Fast Eddie's" last season with the Italian team.

Emerson Fittipaldi, the first Brazilian Formula One world champion.

Ayrton Senna has been revered like a saint in Brazil since his tragic death at the Imola circuit in 1994.

Nelson Piquet, above, was three times Formula One world champion in the 1980s.

Rubens Barrichello, left, is still struggling to emerge from the long shadow of his friend and mentor Ayrton Senna.

Barrichello and the boys from Brazil

BRAZIL HAS A LONG TRADITION of excellence in motor sport. With football, it is one of the few things that unites the Brazilian people. Accordingly, expectations are high, and this has put enormous pressure on Stewart-Ford driver Rubens Barrichello, the country's current standard-bearer in Formula One.

Brazilian champions
The first great Brazilian Formula One driver was Emerson Fittipaldi, who won world championships in 1972 and 1974, fighting against drivers of the calibre of Jackie Stewart and Niki Lauda. It is arguable that only his move to the inferior Copersucar team, run by his brother Wilson, prevented further world championship victories.

Fittipaldi then moved to IndyCars, where he further demonstrated his worth, continuing to win races well into the 1990s.

Nelson Piquet was the next Brazilian to clinch the Formula One championship in 1981, driving for Brabham. Although some critics claimed that his victories owed much to superior machinery, the fact that he won two further championships in 1983 and 1987 was convincing proof of his superb skills.

Senna the great
The fame of Fittipaldi and Piquet was all but eclipsed, however, by Ayrton Senna. His record of 64 poles, 41 grand prix wins, and three world championships was outstanding. There can be little doubt that he

would have overtaken Alain Prost's record of 51 wins had he not been killed at San Marino in 1994. His fellow drivers believed him to be one of the all-time greats, and in Brazil he is venerated as a near-god.

Out of the shadow
Barrichello came into Formula One in 1993, in Senna's last full season. He regarded Senna as both a friend and a mentor. Only recently has he shaken off the long shadow cast by his hero's achievements.

From the age of six, when he began driving go-carts, Barrichello wanted to be a racer. Fuelled by self-belief – and the sponsorship of the Brazilian food-industry giant Arisco – his rise through the ranks was meteoric, and he was snapped up

by Eddie Jordan at the age of 20. His future looked bright.

After a relatively good year in 1994, however, he seemed to lose his way. He left Jordan in 1997 for Stewart, a new team facing the pitfalls of breaking into Formula One. It was not until this season that Stewart made real progress, thanks to an improved chassis, a new engine – and the new-found confidence of their lead driver.

Rubens on a roll
In Melbourne, Barrichello fought from the back of the grid to finish fifth, and he led the race in Brazil. He is enjoying himself: "This is the best season I have had," he says. Brazil may be about to find the new hero that it craves.

2 MAY • IMOLA

San Marino Grand Prix

For the first time in 16 years, Ferrari had a victory to celebrate on their home circuit, thanks to the extraordinary skills of Michael Schumacher. But most of the talk after the race was not so much about how Schumacher had won as how David Coulthard had lost, after leading at the wheel of a quicker car. The Scot blamed back markers, especially Olivier Panis and Pedro Diniz, who had blocked his path as he tried to lap them. Yet, for McLaren, with only one win in the first three races of the season, excuses were starting to wear thin.

Schumacher raises his fist in salute after his first win of the season.

The Circuit

The Autodromo Enzo and Dino Ferrari at Imola has undergone extreme change since 1994, the year when Ayrton Senna and Roland Ratzenberger were killed on the circuit. Chicanes have tamed the Tamburello and Villeneuve curves, while the Variante Bassa corner has been made less extreme. The circuit now puts a heavy strain on transmission, brakes, and tyres.

Track length 4.929 km (3.063 miles)

Race distance 305.598 km (189.895 miles) — 62 laps

1998 winner David Coulthard, McLaren-Mercedes

Lap record 1:25.531 min, Heinz-Harald Frentzen, Williams-Renault, 1997

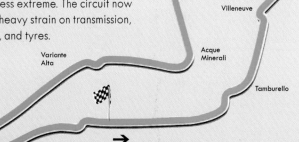

Race Result

	Driver	Time
1	M. Schumacher	1:33:44.792
2	Coulthard	1:33:49.057
3	Barrichello	1 lap behind
4	Hill	1 lap behind
5	Fisichella	1 lap behind
6	Alesi	1 lap behind

Drivers' Championship

	Driver	Points
1	M. Schumacher	16
2	Irvine	12
3	Hakkinen	10
	=Frentzen	10
5	R. Schumacher	7
6	Barrichello	6
	=Coulthard	6
8	Fisichella	5
9	Hill	3
10	Herbert	2

De la Rosa, Panis, Alesi, 1 point.

Constructors' Championship

	Constructor	Points
1	Ferrari	28
2	McLaren-Mercedes	16
3	Jordan-Mugen-Honda	13
4	Williams-Supertec	7
5	Stewart-Ford	6
6	Benetton-Playlife	5

Arrows, Prost-Peugeot, Sauber, 1 point.

Smart Schuey steals the show

Qualification

For the third successive occasion, Hakkinen and Coulthard delivered a one-two for McLaren in qualifying. On the circuit where he won in 1998, Coulthard ran his Finnish team-mate very close, but still missed pole position. Schumacher outstripped his colleague, Irvine, by almost half a second, as Ferrari took possession of the second row of the grid.

Canadian comeback

With a superb drive, former world champion Jacques Villeneuve took fifth place, hinting that a revival in his fortunes was in sight. As in Melbourne and São Paulo, Barrichello made the top six for Stewart. The Williams cars continued to disappoint, slower than the Jordans of Frentzen and Hill.

Benetton had a most dismal session. Fisichella and Wurz qualified 16th and 17th respectively, the worst qualifying performance by a United Colours team in their entire 16 years of Formula One competition. Finnish driver Mika Salo also had a depressing time after being called on by BAR at the last minute as a substitute for the injured Ricardo Zonta. Salo could only qualify a lowly 19th, recording a time more than two seconds slower than his colleague Villeneuve.

Qualifying Times

1 Hakkinen	McLaren-Mercedes	1:26.362
2 Coulthard	McLaren-Mercedes	1:26.384
3 M. Schumacher	Ferrari	1:26.538
4 Irvine	Ferrari	1:26.993
5 Villeneuve	BAR-Supertec	1:27.313
6 Barrichello	Stewart-Ford	1:27.409
7 Frentzen	Jordan-Mugen-Honda	1:27.613
8 Hill	Jordan-Mugen-Honda	1:27.708
9 R. Schumacher	Williams-Supertec	1:27.770
10 Zanardi	Williams-Supertec	1:28.142
11 Panis	Prost-Peugeot	1:28.205
12 Herbert	Stewart-Ford	1:28.246
13 Alesi	Sauber-Petronas	1:28.253
14 Trulli	Prost-Peugeot	1:28.403
15 Diniz	Sauber-Petronas	1:28.599
16 Fisichella	Benetton-Playlife	1:28.750
17 Wurz	Benetton-Playlife	1:28.765
18 De la Rosa	Arrows	1:29.293
19 Salo	BAR-Supertec	1:29.451
20 Takagi	Arrows	1:29.656
21 Gené	Minardi-Ford	1:30.035
22 Badoer	Minardi-Ford	1:30.945

According to Michael Schumacher, "It's always a good feeling to be driving around Imola when you drive a Ferrari." It was an especially good feeling this year, with a victory that put Schuey at the top of the drivers' table and Ferrari out in front in the constructors' title race.

The grand prix began with McLaren building on their impressive performance in qualifying. Hakkinen set off at a blistering pace with Coulthard in pursuit, the Finnish driver opening up a 13-second lead over his Scottish team-mate. Schumacher, meanwhile, was biding his time, tucked in to third position, waiting for the McLarens to give him a chance.

Driver error

On lap 17, with the race apparently solidly in his grasp, Hakkinen inexplicably rode over the kerb and crashed into the barrier opposite the pits on the start-finish straight. The driver climbed out shamefaced in front of the Mercedes-Benz chief executive, Jurgen Hubbert, who was on the McLaren pit wall, and of thousands of flag-waving Ferrari *tifosi*. "Drivers don't like to admit they made a mistake," Hakkinen said later, "but I just lost it."

Superior tactics

Coulthard inherited the lead, but Schumacher looked increasingly like a hunter stalking his prey. As so often, the Ferrari tacticians seem to have thought out their race more clearly. Schumacher was called in for the first of two stops on lap 31. Caught up in traffic, Coulthard failed to capitalize, and when the Scot went in for his single pit-stop on lap 35, Schumacher seized the lead.

This was the start of agony and frustration for Coulthard. He came out of the pit lane behind not only Schumacher, but also back markers Panis, Fisichella, and Diniz. Despite being shown the blue flag, the back markers failed to move over to be lapped. Assailed by McLaren boss

Schumacher: "I told you so."

Ron Dennis, Alain Prost eventually instructed Panis to let Coulthard through — only for the Scot to slide off and be passed by Panis once again. While this nightmare went on behind him, Schumacher progressed with pace and assurance, carving through

Setback for Villeneuve

Trouble at BAR: Jacques Villeneuve, left, and team boss Craig Pollock talk it over.

On Saturday, Jacques Villeneuve and the whole BAR camp were optimistic after the former world champion qualified for the third row of the grid. Villeneuve described himself as "very excited" by the improvement in his car's performance. So he was bitterly disappointed when his gears failed at the start of the race. "We have to make sure that things like this don't happen again," he said. No BAR car has yet finished a race.

Coulthard slides off the track, losing more precious seconds in the course of his frustrated pursuit of Schumacher.

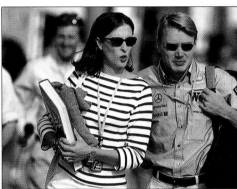

Irvine shows his speed, above, before engine failure brought his race to a premature end.

Hakkinen with his wife at Imola: the Finnish driver always looks coolly confident, despite setbacks.

back-marker traffic with apparent ease. Once the Ferrari number one emerged from his second stop in the lead, the race was as good as won.

Behind the leaders, the Stewart team once more looked impressive. Barrichello inherited the third spot on the podium after Irvine's engine blew, and Herbert was heading for a good fifth place before, with his habitual ill-fortune, suffering a late mechanical failure. Hill won back some pride after recent poor performances with a hard-working fourth place.

But the day belonged to Ferrari and to Schumacher. The German driver said: "After such a long time without a victory, it was a great feeling to deliver the wishes of the fans...I enjoyed going round slowly afterwards, looking into the faces of the people. I was soaking it up."

BETWEEN THE RACES

4 May BMW-Williams on track for the new millennium

BMW Motorsport director Gerhard Berger has declared himself "very satisfied" with the first trials of a BMW-Williams test car. A Williams FW20 mounting a new BMW V10 engine was driven for 480 km (300 miles) by test driver Jörg Muller at the Miramas track, near Marseilles in southern France, last week. Williams are scheduled to race with the BMW V10 in the year 2000.

The engine has been developed at Grove, Oxfordshire, under the technical direction of Paul Rosche, an experienced engineer who was responsible for the BMW engine that powered Nelson Piquet to the world championship in a Brabham in 1983. Rosche and his team have been working on the engine since early 1997. Its development has been shrouded in secrecy, but rumours suggest that there have been some serious problems on the test bed.

The Munich-based firm are heavily committed to a successful return to Formula One. They last supplied a Formula One engine in 1988, to the Arrows team.

6 May Teams set to ditch Supertec

There are currently three teams using the Renault-Mecachrome engines supplied by Super Performance Competition Engineering — Supertec for short. Williams, Benetton, and BAR have paid top money for the privilege of an engine that appears to be leaving them short of power.

It has long been known that Williams are shifting to BMW next year. Recently, BAR have begun lining up a deal with Honda. And now Benetton are angling for a tie-up with Renault. This would leave Supertec with no customers, except possibly Arrows, who are known to be dissatisfied with their current engine.

However, Supertec's manager, Flavio Briatore, may not be overly concerned. Both BAR and Benetton have signed contracts that commit them to taking engines from Supertec for next season. It is reckoned that they will each have to pay Supertec around $20 million in 2000, even if they switch to another engine supplier.

The Brands Hatch circuit in Kent has an illustrious history, but it has not hosted a Formula One grand prix since 1986.

11 May F1 for the USA

It has been confirmed that there will be an American Grand Prix in next year's Formula One calendar. The race will be held on 24 September on a specially constructed circuit at the Indianapolis speedway, home of the Indy 500.

12 May Prost denies Peugeot rift

Alain Prost is playing down rumours of a dispute with engine suppliers Peugeot, after his team's disappointing start to this year's campaign. The gossip was that Prost and Peugeot Sport boss, Corrado Provera, had clashed over Prost's criticisms of the Peugeot V10. Prost is alleged to have expressed an interest in switching to a Honda engine.

Claiming his remarks had been distorted, Prost said: "It is true that Peugeot does not yet have an engine at the top level, but it is the best behind Mercedes and Ford." Peugeot are known to be working on a new, lighter engine for the 2000 season.

12 May Get out of our way!

Michael Schumacher has joined David Coulthard in criticism of back markers who may have cost the Scotsman victory at Imola. Coulthard is reckoned to have lost 10 seconds trying to lap drivers who failed to move over.

Schumacher had much greater success carving his way through the traffic, but he spelled out his concern at some drivers' behaviour. "The rule is that they must move over at the first opportunity," he said, stressing that failure to observe this rule could be not only irritating, but also dangerous as well.

McLaren boss Ron Dennis defended Coulthard against accusations that he had been too cautious. "If David had gone off trying to get past two back markers," Dennis said, "he would have been an idiot."

14 May British Grand Prix on the move

A deal struck between Bernie Ecclestone and Nicola Foulston, chief executive of Brands Hatch Leisure, should mean that the British Grand Prix moves from its current home at Silverstone to the Brands Hatch circuit in Kent from 2002. Brands Hatch has not hosted a Formula One event since 1986.

Determined to take over the grand prix, Foulston originally bid to buy Silverstone from its owners, the British Racing Drivers' Club (BRDC), whose members include such famous names as

Millionaire Nicola Foulston, the prime mover behind the upheaval in British Formula One.

Stirling Moss, Jody Scheckter, and Damon Hill. When the BRDC rejected a deal last month, Foulston fell back on negotiations with Ecclestone to take the grand prix to Brands Hatch.

Under the current contract, the BRDC will continue to stage the grand prix at Silverstone until 2001. By then Foulston intends to have transformed Brands Hatch into a modern Formula

Bernie's digital TV circus

One circuit at an estimated cost of £20 million. The work is going to be entrusted to the German company Tilke GmbH, which recently built the Sepang circuit outside Kuala Lumpur that will stage the Malaysian Grand Prix later this season.

BRDC spokesmen are still casting doubt on the move from Silverstone, suggesting that Brands Hatch will not have the facilities to stage a grand prix. Ecclestone, on the other hand, has expressed his "100 per cent confidence" in Brands Hatch as a Formula One venue. He seems determined to break the power of the BRDC, even threatening to remove the British Grand Prix from the race calendar rather than see the current situation continue.

Foulston will pay the FIA around £50 million for the right to stage the event for six years. This is a sum that the BRDC cannot hope to match.

Bernie Ecclestone, Formula One wheeler-dealer.

BERNIE ECCLESTONE HAS NEVER been a man to do things by halves. He is said to have invested $100 million in the pay-per-view digital television service that now offers subscribers in some European countries Formula One coverage of unprecedented quality. With on-board pictures from every car, as well as some 80 trackside cameras, Ecclestone's operation seems to be the fulfilment of every armchair petrolhead's dreams.

On the road

The logistics of TV coverage on this scale are mindblowing. A studio large enough to house 120 staff, complete with its own generators, canteen and air-conditioning, not to mention the mass of television equipment, has to be transported to different parts of the globe every two weeks at the height of the season. For Asia and South America, the studio travels on two Boeing cargo jets. In Europe, it is packed on to a convoy of 25 identical Mercedes transporter trucks.

It takes two days to assemble the studio after it arrives at the grand prix site. The end result looks like an aircraft hangar. To insiders it is known as "Bakersville", after Eddie Baker, who runs the operation for Ecclestone.

As of 1999, the service is available to subscribers in Germany, Italy, France, and Scandanavia. It will not be long before other countries, including the UK, are linked up. There are still observers who doubt whether enough enthusiasts will be ready to pay for the service that Ecclestone has to offer.

But Ecclestone himself is full of faith and pride in his new enterprise. "This operation is the only one of its kind in the world," he said. And he added, "You won't watch sports live in a few years unless it's on digital."

ITV's Formula One studio – the terrestrial channels cannot match the quality of digital coverage.

The fleet of Mercedes trucks that carry the mobile digital studio.

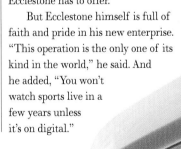

Monaco Grand Prix

This year Ferrari painted the town red as their cars achieved the team's first ever one-two victory at Monaco. After qualifying it looked as though the race might be an even contest between McLaren and Ferrari, but within seconds of the start the Ferrari drivers had made their bid for all-out victory.

The tight, twisty circuit suited the Ferraris, while the more powerful McLarens found handling a problem. But it was a race as much about drivers as cars, and in the end Schumacher came out on top. It was his 16th grand prix win for Ferrari, making him the most successful driver in the Scuderia's history.

Schumacher negotiates the tight bends of the world's most spectacular circuit.

Track length 3.366 km (2.092 miles)
Race distance 262.599 km (163.176 miles) — 78 laps
1998 winner Mika Hakkinen, McLaren-Mercedes
Lap record 1:22.948 min, Mika Hakkinen, McLaren-Mercedes, 1998

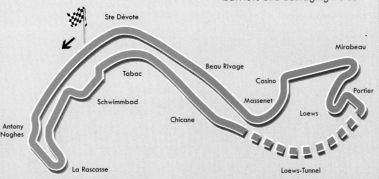

The Circuit

The narrow and winding street-circuit race that runs through the centre of Monaco is one of the high points of the grand prix calendar. No other circuit demands such a high level of concentration and such an acute degree of driver sensitivity. With hardly any run-off areas, the slightest mistake can result in the driver colliding with the crash barriers and damaging his car.

Race Result

	Driver	Time
1	M. Schumacher	1:49:31.812
2	Irvine	1:50:02.288
3	Hakkinen	1:50:09.295
4	Frentzen	1:50:25.821
5	Fisichella	1 lap behind
6	Wurz	1 lap behind

Drivers' Championship

	Driver	Points
1	M. Schumacher	26
2	Irvine	18
3	Hakkinen	14
4	Frentzen	13
5	R. Schumacher	7
	=Fisichella	7
7	Coulthard	6
	=Barrichello	6
9	Hill	3

De la Rosa, Panis, Alesi, Wurz, 1 point.

Constructors' Championship

	Constructor	Points
1	Ferrari	44
2	McLaren-Mercedes	20
3	Jordan-Mugen-Honda	16
4	Benetton-Playlife	8
5	Williams-Supertec	7
6	Stewart-Ford	6
7	Arrows	1
	=Prost-Peugeot	1
	=Sauber-Petronas	1

A record-breaking victory for Ferrari

Qualification

Saturday's qualifying showed that Monaco is a circuit that benefits the Ferrari F399. Through most of the hour-long session, the Ferraris had the edge over the competition, and Schumacher was sure he had pole in his grasp

Circuit breaker

In the final few minutes, however, the Ferraris and McLarens came out on track again and everything was reversed. To Schumacher's irritation, Hakkinen stormed through all three sections and just pipped the German driver to pole. Coulthard, who had been 13th in the first day's practice session, also spoiled Ferrari's day by beating Irvine into fourth on the grid. Ferrari subsequently complained that Hakkinen had ignored a yellow flag during his final lap, but the race stewards overruled the protest.

Back of the field

The first four drivers were all within a half second of each other, reflecting the dominance of McLaren and Ferrari. Of the rest, Rubens Barrichello had a good session, his Stewart gaining fifth place just ahead of the Jordan of Heinz-Harald Frentzen. Villeneuve showed his mastery of the circuit by coaxing his BAR to a highly creditable eighth place, but given its previous unreliability, would it last the race?

Qualifying Times

1	Hakkinen	McLaren-Mercedes	1:20.547
2	M Schumacher	Ferrari	1:20.611
3	Coulthard	McLaren-Mercedes	1:20.956
4	Irvine	Ferrari	1:21.011
5	Barrichello	Stewart-Ford	1:21.530
6	Frentzen	Jordan-Mugen-Honda	1:21.556
7	Trulli	Prost-Peugeot	1:21.769
8	Villeneuve	BAR-Supertec	1:21.827
9	Fisichella	Benetton-Playlife	1:21.938
10	Wurz	Benetton-Playlife	1:21.968
11	Zanardi	Williams-Supertec	1:22.152
12	Salo	BAR-Supertec	1:22.241
13	Herbert	Stewart-Ford	1:22.248
14	Alesi	Sauber-Petronas	1:22.354
15	Diniz	Sauber-Petronas	1:22.659
16	R Schumacher	Williams-Supertec	1:22.719
17	Hill	Jordan-Mugen-Honda	1:22.832
18	Panis	Prost-Peugeot	1:22.916
19	Takagi	Arrows	1:23.290
20	Badoer	Minardi-Ford	1:23.765
21	De la Rosa	Arrows	1:24.260
22	Gené	Minardi-Ford	1:24.914

Monaco may be an "impossible circuit" with a narrow and winding track that inhibits overtaking, and a lack of space that prevents the teams from operating effectively in the pit lane. But as the glamour circuit of the season it has a special place in the hearts of racing enthusiasts. No driver forgets winning here. Last year Hakkinen regarded his victory as one of the high points of his career. And the jubilation of Schumacher as he crossed the line this year told its own story: Ferrari were back on top.

Ferrari supporters occupy floating trackside seats in Monte Carlo.

By the end of the first corner the fight for supremacy at Monaco had been decided. Hakkinen, in pole position, was slow in getting away, whereas Schumacher shot forward the moment the red lights went out. The McLaren tried to edge Schumacher off his line, but the Ferrari was quicker and at the first corner it had nosed ahead. Locking his brakes, Hakkinen conceded and Schumacher raced up the hill in the lead. It was a lead he would keep to the chequered flag.

Successful strategy

Schumacher's quick start, the decisive move of the race, was the result of careful advance planning by the Ferrari team. Guessing that Hakkinen would have a fairly heavy fuel load, to give him the option of staying out as long as possible before his single pit-stop, Ferrari gave Schumacher a lighter fuel load, thus providing him with a crucial speed advantage in the

vital first few seconds of the race. Also, to make doubly sure that their driver would get away like a bullet, Ferrari had flown Schumacher back to the test track at Fiorano on Friday, the traditional Monaco rest day. There he was able to try out a variety of starts with the Bridgestone tyres he had used at Thursday's practice session.

One-two lead

The start was a total Ferrari victory, as Irvine, fourth on the grid, was able to get past Coulthard on the first corner. Coulthard had one of his unlucky days. Although he was able to keep up with the Ferrari number two for most of the race, he was forced to abandon

Right: Schumacher and Irvine celebrate the Ferrari double.

Below: Into the first bend, Schumacher cuts in front of Hakkinen and Irvine squeezes Coulthard into fourth position.

on lap 37 with gearbox failure. McLaren's bad luck continued when Hakkinen lost grip after hitting oil on the track caused by the blow-up of Toro Takagi's engine on lap 36. Hakkinen was forced into the run-off at Mirabeau, and lost around 18 seconds as a result. This allowed Irvine to assume second place when the McLaren driver pitted on lap 50.

Jordan's mixed fortunes

Heinz-Harald Frentzen had another good and careful race. He spent the first part of the race behind Rubens Barrichello, until suspension problems caused the Brazilian to drop back, letting the Jordan driver through for fourth place. Frentzen's Jordan

renaissance was balanced by the decline of his team-mate. After a poor showing in qualifying left him near the back of the grid, Damon Hill tried to force his way through the pack. As a result, he clipped Ralf Schumacher's Williams in an over-optimistic passing manoeuvre and spun out of the race with just three laps completed.

The Benettons exceeded most expectations and picked up the tail-end of the points, with Fisichella coming in ahead of Wurz.

But in the final analysis the race belonged to Ferrari. Schumacher cruised to the finish, followed by his faithful lieutenant Irvine a half-minute behind. It was Schumacher's fourth win at Monaco in six years.

Fizzy provides sparkle for Benetton

Since Schumacher left in 1996, Benetton have under-performed in a big way. Uncertain handling and a poor powerplant were blamed as

chief culprits. Lack of commitment from previous Benetton drivers was also a part of the equation, but this charge cannot be laid at the door of Giancarlo Fisichella. His enthusiasm and driving skill have been plus-points for the team. He failed to finish in Brazil as a result of clutch failure, but since then he has been consistently in the points – a real achievement for a team currently in transition.

Fisichella on his way to fifth place in Monaco.

BETWEEN THE RACES

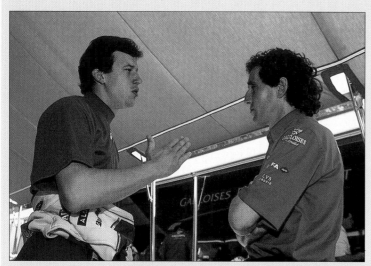

Olivier Panis, left, does not always see eye-to-eye with his team boss Alain Prost.

19 May Panis blasted by Prost

Tensions within the Prost camp have surfaced with outspoken criticism of driver Olivier Panis by team chief Alain Prost. The former world champion was angry that Panis failed to let David Coulthard pass him during this month's San Marino Grand Prix, despite being shown the blue flag. Prost described Panis's driving as "not good enough". There are rumours that this may be Panis's last season with the Prost team.

21 May Honda confirms deals with BAR and Jordan

Confirming rumours that appeared in the sports press in April, Japanese car giant Honda announced today that they have signed an agreement to supply works engines and chassis technology to BAR from the start of next season. The Honda-BAR partnership will initially run for three years. It replaces Honda's earlier plan to create their own Formula One organization that would have become the 12th team on the grid in 2000.

At the same time, Honda confirmed that they would continue to supply Jordan with engines from its associate company, Mugen, at least until the end of the 2001 season. The Mugen-Honda engine will be of equal specification to the Honda works engine. Eddie Jordan welcomed the decision, saying it would provide his team with "the stability it requires to mount an even stronger world championship challenge."

It is rumoured that the 12th team spot left vacant by Honda may be filled by Lotus, one of the most famous names in

Formula One history. Bernie Ecclestone is believed to favour a revival of the Lotus team, which collapsed under a heavy burden of debt in 1994.

26 May Verstappen looks for a team

Honda's decision not to set up their own team was bad news for Dutch driver Jos Verstappen. Given the job of testing the new Honda car, he had clocked up such quick times that he seemed certain to be signed up for the team on their re-entry into Formula One. He will now be hoping that another team needs his services.

Sir Frank Williams, coping with disappointment this year.

27 May Williams anniversary blues

On the threshold of his 400th grand prix as a Formula One constructor, Sir Frank Williams has little to celebrate, with his team occupying a modest fifth place in the championship. The Williams technical director, Patrick Head, admitted that, although it was not impossible Williams might win a race this season, "I don't think many people will be putting money on us." Head blamed the team's lack of success on its uncompetitive engine.

27 May Coulthard hits back at press criticism

In the British magazine *Motoring News*, McLaren driver David Coulthard has attacked the press for its criticism of his driving skills and of his alleged lack of assertiveness. "I understand that the people in the press have their job to do," he said, "but I don't think it should be under question whether I deserve a drive with a top team or not."

28 May Hill claims that he is here to stay

Former world champion Damon Hill today described reports that he intended to retire at the end of the current season as "premature and predictable". Hill is 38 years old and has had a poor start to the season, finishing only one of four races so far.

However, according to Hill, the Jordan team has remained "very supportive". This was confirmed by Eddie Jordan, who said: "You write off Damon at your peril."

29 May Ecclestone bond issue is a billion dollar success

Bernie Ecclestone's plans to float Formula One on the stock market are alive again after a successful Eurobond issue that raised $1.4 billion for his family trust. The bond issue was handled by Morgan Stanley and the Westdeutsche Landesbank on the Luxembourg stock exchange.

The bond issue demonstrated the confidence of financial institutions in the money-making potential of Formula One – a confidence that was lacking last year when Ecclestone's initial plans to float Formula One stalled. Investors were apparently not put off by an investigation of Ecclestone's business currently being conducted by agencies of the EU.

In the light of the bond issue, Ecclestone said that a stock market flotation of Formula One would probably occur within three years.

Double world champion Niki Lauda in his Ferrari.

Blue flags and back markers

A track marshal waves the blue flag indicating the driver should move over.

AFTER AS LITTLE AS 20 LAPS from the start, the lead drivers may find themselves behind back markers, who will be driving several seconds a lap slower than the leaders. Often, the back markers will be fighting with each other to gain better track positions and are unaware of the arrival of the leaders' cars. Hence the introduction of blue flags, which are waved at back markers to instruct them to let the lead cars overtake swiftly and safely.

Haven't got the blues

As overtaking has become more difficult, the need for back markers to heed the marshals' blue flags has become more important than ever. Increasingly, however, the top drivers have complained at what they see as the back markers' refusal to move over. Their complaints came to a head at Monaco, following events at the San Marino Grand Prix. Michael Schumacher criticized the lack of enforcement over the blue flag rule, which states that if a driver fails to move over after seeing three blue flags he faces a ten-second stop-go penalty. "This rule doesn't seem to exist any more," said Schumacher. "It has not been enforced for a while and drivers notice that. It needs to be enforced so they move immediately."

Tightening up

These criticisms, expressed to race director Charlie Whiting, led to a tightening of the enforcement of the blue flag rule. In addition, the blue flag warnings are now shown on the timing monitors throughout the pit lane. This tells the teams that the warning has been given and that they should tell their driver to move over.

McLaren's David Coulthard, who had suffered most at the hands of back markers at San Marino, even went so far as to recommend the imposition of personal fines on the errant drivers to "hit them in the pocket". Believing he had lost the race to Schumacher because of Panis's intransigence, Coulthard's bitterness was understandable.

Schuey overtakes Lauda as Ferrari champ

HIS VICTORY IN MONTE CARLO was Michael Schumacher's 16th win for Ferrari, making him the most successful driver in the Italian team's history. The previous record holder was Niki Lauda.

Schumacher was pleased with his new record. "Being a Ferrari driver already means something special," he said. "Winning races for Ferrari is super-special, and being the most successful Ferrari driver is one more on top of that."

Something missing

Schumacher's ranking as the top Ferrari driver ever will not be universally accepted, however, unless he manages to win the team a world championship. He came agonizingly close to it in 1997 and 1998, but near-misses count for little. Lauda, by contrast, won two drivers' world championships for Ferrari, in 1975 and 1977.

Renaissance man

Schumacher has played a key role in the Ferrari renaissance of the late 1990s, but the question of winning the championship continues to obsess him – and the Ferrari team. Although Schumacher said the record number of wins would be "a nice statistic" to look back on in retirement, he also said that it was "more important to win the race for the championship". Ferrari would no doubt agree.

Schumacher, left, celebrates what has been a Ferrari success story so far.

Spanish Grand Prix

Although the McLaren team dominated the Spanish Grand Prix, the race will really be remembered not for their success, but as a notorious example of what is wrong with Formula One. It provided ammunition for those critics who believe that the sport has become little more than a succession of cars going round in circles, albeit with a lot of noise. During the entire race of 65 laps there were only two overtaking manoeuvres, and the outcome was decided by mechanical failures and pit-stops. McLaren were, of course, delighted with the points they won. They had been soundly beaten in Monaco, and Spain was their revenge. It was an especially disappointing race for Eddie Irvine, who outpaced team-mate Michael Schumacher in qualifying, but started poorly from the front of the grid and eventually finished fourth.

Hakkinen takes the lead at the start, while Coulthard holds off the two Ferraris and Villeneuve sprints forward on the outside.

The Circuit

A number of high-speed bends at the Circuit de Catalunya ensure that drivers are called upon to demonstrate their physical fitness. Although the circuit is demanding, it has good run-off areas and from a safety point of view it is popular with the drivers. The cars are subject to high levels of fuel consumption and tyre wear, the latter a consequence of the track's highly abrasive surface. The drivers are very familiar with the circuit because it is used for winter testing.

Track length 4.728 km (2.938 miles)
Race distance 307.328 km (190.97 miles) – 65 laps
1998 winner Mika Hakkinen, McLaren-Mercedes
Lap record 1:22.242 min, Giancarlo Fisichella, Jordan-Peugeot, 1997

Race Result

	Driver	Time
1	Hakkinen	1:34:13.665
2	Coulthard	1:34:19.903
3	M. Schumacher	1:34:24.510
4	Irvine	1:34:43.847
5	R. Schumacher	1:35:40.873
6	Trulli	1 lap behind

Drivers' Championship

	Driver	Points
1	M. Schumacher	30
2	Hakkinen	24
3	Irvine	21
4	Frentzen	13
5	Coulthard	12
6	R. Schumacher	9
7	Fisichella	7
8	Barrichello	6
9	Hill	3

De la Rosa, Panis, Alesi, Wurz, Trulli, 1 pt.

Constructors' Championship

	Constructor	Points
1	Ferrari	51
2	McLaren-Mercedes	35
3	Jordan-Mugen-Honda	16
4	Williams-Supertec	9
5	Benetton-Playlife	8
6	Stewart-Ford	6
7	Prost-Peugeot	2
8	Arrows	1
	=Sauber-Petronas	1

Grey procession nets McLaren the points

Qualification

Irvine qualified for the front of the grid.

For a driver of the calibre of Michael Schumacher, not to make pole is disappointing, but to be fourth and two places behind your racing lieutenant is vexatious in the extreme. No matter what his engineer, Ignazio Lunetta, suggested, Schumacher just couldn't solve the problem.

Irvine had driven like a demon, but with minutes remaining Hakkinen raced over the line ahead of the Ferrari number two. Coulthard considered himself unlucky not to have run in behind the Finn, and had to content himself with being sandwiched between the Ferraris. Sauber's Alesi had an impressive drive to secure a place on the third row just ahead of Villeneuve. The times for the front-runners were tight, the first eight all achieving their best lap within the 1:22 mark.

Qualifying Times

1 Hakkinen	McLaren-Mercedes	1:22.088
2 Irvine	Ferrari	1:22.219
3 Coulthard	McLaren-Mercedes	1:22.244
4 M. Schumacher	Ferrari	1:22.277
5 Alesi	Sauber-Petronas	1:22.388
6 Villeneuve	BAR-Supertec	1:22.703
7 Barrichello	Stewart-Ford	1:22.920
8 Frentzen	Jordan-Mugen-Honda	1:22.938
9 Trulli	Prost-Peugeot	1:23.194
10 R. Schumacher	Williams-Supertec	1:23.303
11 Hill	Jordan-Mugen-Honda	1:23.317
12 Diniz	Sauber-Petronas	1:23.331
13 Fisichella	Benetton-Playlife	1:23.333
14 Herbert	Stewart-Ford	1:23.505
15 Panis	Prost-Peugeot	1:23.559
16 Salo	BAR-Supertec	1:23.683
17 Zanardi	Williams-Supertec	1:23.703
18 Wurz	Benetton-Playlife	1:23.824
19 De la Rosa	Arrows	1:24.619
20 Takagi	Arrows	1:25.280
21 Gené	Minardi-Ford	1:25.672
22 Badoer	Minardi-Ford	1:25.833

The Ferrari demolition job at Monaco put the pressure firmly onto McLaren. The Woking-based team responded in their typical way with a full house of 16 points. But as a race it was no spectacle. Irvine summed up his day's work: "I wish I'd had my stereo in the car to keep me amused."

Part of the reason why the race in Barcelona was so dull is that the teams do much of their testing at the Circuit de Catalunya. The race technicians' laptops are crammed with analyses of how their cars behave on this circuit in nearly all possible circumstances. They know it so well that there can be few surprises.

Leapfrog start

Perhaps the only real upset of the day happened at the start when Jacques Villeneuve caught the front-runners by surprise, vaulting from sixth to third as the red lights went out. In marked contrast to the situation in the previous race at Monaco, the two McLarens made excellent starts while the two Ferraris stumbled. Irvine was the main culprit, blocking his team leader before the first corner. This allowed Villeneuve to go round the two Ferraris on the outside, leaving Schumacher fourth and Irvine fifth.

The pattern is set

These few seconds set the pattern of the race as Villeneuve held up Schumacher and the rest of the pack, opening the door for Hakkinen and Coulthard to build up a comfortable lead. That Villeneuve was able to fend off the Ferraris in his underpowered BAR was a tribute to his tenacity and skill as a driver. Schumacher made an attempt to get past the Canadian at Turn 5 on the first lap, but soon accepted that discretion was the better part of valour and decided to wait for the pit-stops to get ahead.

On lap 24 both Villeneuve and Schumacher came into the pit lane. Thanks to the Ferrari mechanics, Schumacher got out first, and to add

The McLaren crew in the pits — exciting action on a dull day.

A familiar sight: Hakkinen leads and Coulthard follows.

insult to injury Villeneuve also found himself behind Irvine who had pitted two laps earlier. Villeneuve continued to race on, but on lap 40 his gearbox went and the BAR car once again failed to deliver.

With BAR's Villeneuve out of commission, Schumacher set about chasing down both of the McLaren drivers. Fortunately for Schumacher, a poor pit-stop by Coulthard, who

carelessly over-shot the stop point, allowed the top German driver to close on the second-placed McLaren.

Schuey's frustration

It was a fine piece of driving by Schumacher, but during the second round of pit-stops he found himself held up by Tora Takagi. "As well as that," said Schumacher after the race, "my last set of tyres wasn't great, so

*Schumacher takes his revenge on
Mika Hakkinen on the podium.*

my final stint wasn't as good as the
first two. We made adjustments to the
car through the race, and the handling
felt very different from the first to the
second to the third set."

Relief for McLaren

As the race drew to a close Hakkinen
was well out in front and Schumacher
set his sights on taking second place
from Coulthard. Schumacher's chance
came when Coulthard found himself
bogged down by the back markers –
Trulli, Barrichello, and Hill – who
were battling for sixth. The Ferrari
was hot on the McLaren's tail when a
space among the back markers opened
up and Coulthard shot through like a
rocket. He kept tight hold of second
place, crossing the finishing line six
seconds behind Hakkinen.

The result was a McLaren one-
two, giving the team the maximum
16 points. It was an enormous relief
for McLaren. They knew that if they
couldn't win on a track like this,
which suited their cars, then their
dream of retaining the championship
would be doomed. Hakkinen was now
only six points behind Schumacher in
the championship, and McLaren
could look forward to duelling with
Ferrari in Montreal, Canada.

*The procession tours the circuit,
with Villeneuve tucked in between
the McLarens and the Ferraris.*

BETWEEN THE RACES

31 May *Barrichello suffers post-race disqualification*

The Stewart-Ford car driven by Rubens Barrichello in the Spanish Grand Prix has failed a post-race technical inspection. The stewards decided that the fasteners holding the skid plank to the underside of the chassis were too large and constituted a safety hazard. Barrichello has consequently been disqualified, although he had in any case only managed a disappointing eighth place.

31 May *Swedish driver wins Indy prize*

This year's Indianapolis 500, traditionally the top event in the American motor sport season, has been won by Swedish driver Kenny Brack. The winner received $1.4 million of prize money.

North American motor sport remains plagued, however, by the four-year-old split between the IRL (Indy Racing League), and its rival CART (Championship Auto Racing Teams). CART has boycotted the Indy 500 since the IRL took it over in 1996.

CART has announced that it intends to include events outside the United States in its race programme. Germany, in particular, is being sized up as a possible site for future CART races.

FIA boss Max Mosley has taken a tough stance in the dispute over grooved tyres.

2 June *Mosley not impressed by drivers' criticism of rules*

FIA President Max Mosley has responded to criticism of Formula One regulations with a robust defence of the current rules. Michael Schumacher and Damon Hill are among drivers complaining that grooved tyres and narrower chassis have made cars too difficult to drive and rendered overtaking almost impossible.

Mosley told *The Times* newspaper that "as long as the cars are safe, we are not concerned whether the drivers like the cars or not." He accepted that the Spanish Grand Prix had not been an interesting race, but alleged that this was an exceptional case. "The cars are difficult to drive," he said, "but that is why we are supposed to have the best drivers in the world in Formula One."

4 June *Schumacher happy with his partner*

Michael Schumacher has dismissed rumours that he is dissatisfied with the support he receives from Eddie Irvine. "We work very well together," Schumacher said. "Any talk of problems between us is rubbish."

According to some reports, Schumacher had drawn up a "wish list" of drivers he would

prefer to replace Irvine, including Jarno Trulli, Jean Alesi, and Pedro Diniz. But the German driver said his attitude was: "Why change a winning team?"

8 June *Irvine claims he is better than Hakkinen*

Journalists who interview Ferrari driver Eddie Irvine can be sure of some interesting copy, as the Italian magazine *Autosprint* found this week. In an outspoken mood, Irvine liberally criticized his fellow drivers, especially David Coulthard. "Coulthard is in a very weak position," he is reported as saying, "his ratings are going down race after race." Irvine described both Hakkinen and Schumacher as having "major weak points" and claimed that in some ways he was himself "better than Mika".

The Ulster driver appeared to be angling for a place at McLaren next year. But McLaren chief Ron Dennis said he took "great exception" to some of Irvine's remarks and would be "unlikely" to approach him in any eventuality.

10 June *Ecclestone takes sides against Mosley*

Bernie Ecclestone has set himself on a collision course with fellow Formula One boss Max Mosley by endorsing criticisms of FIA safety regulations that have allegedly made overtaking more difficult. Blaming the current grooved tyres for taking the excitement out of the sport,

Ecclestone said: "We must go back to wide, slick tyres to get more grip and more overtaking."

10 June *Ford take control of the Stewart team*

On the day before former world champion driver Jackie Stewart's 60th birthday, Stewart Grand Prix has been bought by its engine manufacturer, Ford, for about £50 million. Although Ford now hold all the equity in the company, Stewart and his son Paul will remain in place as chairman and deputy chairman. It is rumoured that the Stewart-Ford name may soon be changed to Jaguar, as a boost for Ford's luxury car brand.

Ford have been involved with Stewart Grand Prix since it was founded four years ago. The takeover paradoxically has been

Jackie Stewart at 60, still running his team despite the takeover by Ford.

motivated both by success and failure. The limited impact Stewart has made on the points tables has shown that independents cannot compete in contemporary Formula One. But some recent promising performances have suggested that they are capable of challenging the front-runners if given enough financial and technical support.

Explaining the move to the press, Jackie Stewart said: "The way forward in Formula One is to maximize your firepower. We believe that selling to Ford has enabled us to do this." A Ford spokesman said simply: "To win the world championship, it's desirable to own and run the team ourselves."

Kenny Brack of Sweden celebrates his highly lucrative success in the Indianapolis 500.

What's wrong with Formula One?

THE CRITICISMS THAT WERE voiced after the Spanish Grand Prix reflect a growing dissatisfaction with Formula One from those most closely involved with the sport. These critics include drivers, team bosses, technical directors, and motorsports journalists. Many feel that Formula One has lost its way in the wake of new safety regulations designed to reduce speeds.

They shall not pass

The main problem lies in the extreme difficulty of overtaking. The only time when cars can pass each other is at the start or when in the pits. As a result, at Barcelona there were just two instances of overtaking, whereas at Monza in 1971 there were more than a 100 passing manoeuvres.

Today, a driver trying to overtake risks coming off the track or taking off his rival. During this season, drivers have become increasingly cautious. Ferrari's Ross Brawn even admits that he tells Schumacher not to risk overtaking during the opening phase of the race, preferring that he get past competitors during pit-stops.

At a press conference in Spain, Formula One drivers and other team members expressed their misgivings with the present car regulations. There was a consensus that the modern Formula One cars relied far too much on aerodynamic grip and not enough on tyre grip.

Back to slicks

The drivers suggested that slick tyres be reintroduced and that the cars be made wider in order to increase the turbulence behind the car. The reasoning behind this is that the disturbed air would provide a low-pressure tow effect for following cars on long straights, allowing them to overtake with greater ease. The inability of Michael Schumacher's Ferrari to get past the much slower BAR of Jacques Villeneuve in Spain was startling evidence of the poor slipstreaming effect of modern Formula One cars.

Max Mosley, current president of the FIA, has been reluctant to sanction any changes to the rules. A top-level meeting to discuss the regulations is to be held sometime later in the season. It is unlikely to herald radical reforms.

Above, chased by Mansell, Senna locks up his brakes in an epic overtaking contest at Budapest in 1991. Below, Schumacher knocks Coulthard off track in last season's Canadian Grand Prix.

Canadian Grand Prix

Celebrating a victory *that takes him to the top of the Drivers' Championship, Mika Hakkinen is flanked by second-placed Giancarlo Fisichella (left) and Ferrari's Eddie Irvine.*

Canada lived up to its reputation for the unpredictable, much to the relief of the Formula One top brass, Max Mosley and Bernie Ecclestone, who were looking anxiously for an entertaining race after the dull procession of the Spanish Grand Prix. Spectators were thrilled by a race of spins and crashes, in which the safety car did more laps than many of the regular Formula One cars. Michael Schumacher seemed to have the race sewn up until a simple mistake took him out of contention. Finnish driver Mika Hakkinen took maximum advantage of the opportunity offered him, and pushed ahead of his German rival to lead the championship.

Hakkinen made no mistake *once Schumacher's exit had opened up the route to victory. The Finn commented at the end of the race: "Now I love Canada."*

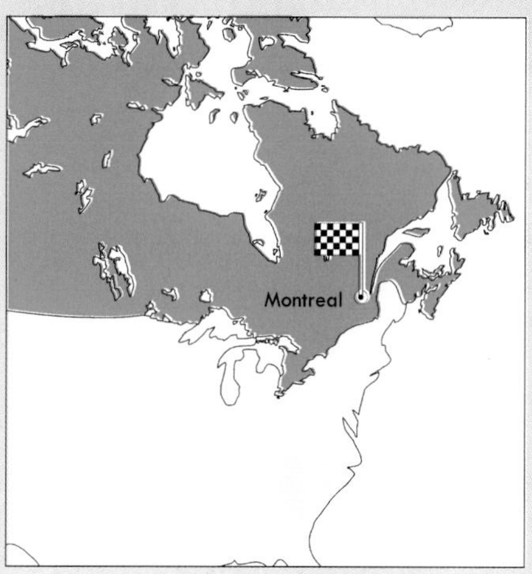

The Circuit

On Montreal's Circuit Gilles Villeneuve, long, high-speed straights alternate with slow chicanes and hairpin bends. This shape of racing circuit puts an especially heavy strain on the brakes. However, the long straights before the bends offer good possibilities for overtaking manoeuvres.

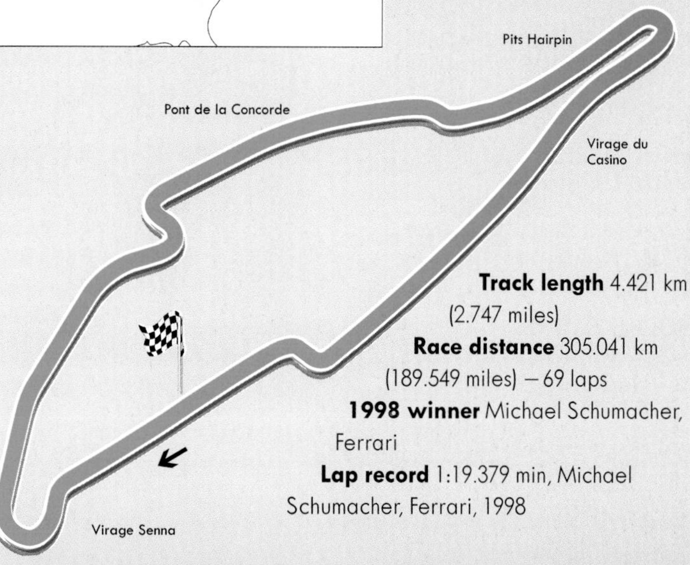

Montreal

Pits Hairpin

Pont de la Concorde

Virage du Casino

Track length 4.421 km (2.747 miles)

Race distance 305.041 km (189.549 miles) — 69 laps

1998 winner Michael Schumacher, Ferrari

Lap record 1:19.379 min, Michael Schumacher, Ferrari, 1998

Virage Senna

Race Result

	Driver	Time
1	Hakkinen	1:41:35.727
2	Fisichella	1:41:36.508
3	Irvine	1:41:37.523
4	R. Schumacher	1:41:38.118
5	Herbert	1:41:38.531
6	Diniz	1:41:39.437

Drivers' Championship

	Driver	Points
1	Hakkinen	34
2	M. Schumacher	30
3	Irvine	25
4	Frentzen	13
=	Fisichella	13
6	Coulthard	12
=	R. Schumacher	12
8	Barrichello	6
9	Hill	3

Herbert, 2 points; De la Rosa, Panis, Alesi, Wurz, Trulli, and Diniz, 1 point.

Constructors' Championship

	Constructor	Points
1	Ferrari	55
2	McLaren-Mercedes	46
3	Jordan-Mugen-Honda	16
4	Williams-Supertec	15
5	Benetton-Playlife	11
6	Stewart-Ford	8
7	Prost-Peugeot	2
=	Sauber-Petronas	2
9	Arrows	1

Schumacher crashes out in thriller

Qualification

Qualifying was dominated by Michael Schumacher's first flying lap, which gained him provisional pole position right at the start of the session. The German then retired to the garage and calmly watched the rest of the field attempt to better his time. They failed, and Schumacher took pole.

For Mika Hakkinen, the whole of the weekend up to qualifying was disappointing. He came seventh on Friday and third on the Saturday morning free practice. Only at the end of qualifying did the Finn find the right balance and pull off the session's second-best time.

Pipped to the pole

Irvine might have got pole, but a final scorching lap was slowed by a spin from Alesi's Sauber, which kept him on the second row. He was joined by Coulthard, who had started the weekend brightly, but faded when it really mattered.

In the middle of the field, the ever-improving Barrichello took fifth place, next to Frentzen, whose team-mate Damon Hill was left languishing in 14th position. Particularly galling for the home fans was Villeneuve's poor showing in 16th place, just ahead of his team-mate Ricardo Zonta.

Qualifying Times

1	M. Schumacher	Ferrari	1:19.298
2	Hakkinen	McLaren-Mercedes	1:19.327
3	Irvine	Ferrari	1:19.440
4	Coulthard	McLaren-Mercedes	1:19.729
5	Barrichello	Stewart-Ford	1:19.930
6	Frentzen	Jordan-Mugen-Honda	1:20.158
7	Fisichella	Benetton-Playlife	1:20.378
8	Alesi	Sauber-Petronas	1:20.459
9	Trulli	Prost-Peugeot	1:20.557
10	Herbert	Stewart-Ford	1:20.829
11	Wurz	Benetton-Playlife	1:21.000
12	Zanardi	Williams-Supertec	1:21.076
13	R. Schumacher	Williams-Supertec	1:21.081
14	Hill	Jordan-Mugen-Honda	1:21.094
15	Panis	Prost-Peugeot	1:21.252
16	Villeneuve	BAR-Supertec	1:21.302
17	Zonta	BAR-Supertec	1:21.467
18	Diniz	Sauber-Petronas	1:21.571
19	Takagi	Arrows	1:21.693
20	De la Rosa	Arrows	1:22.613
21	Badoer	Minardi-Ford	1:22.808
22	Gené	Minardi-Ford	1:23.387

Before the race, Ferrari driver Eddie Irvine expressed a hope that this might be a grand prix to remember: "Just as Barcelona is notorious for being boring, so Montreal has a name for being exciting," he said. With numerous spin-offs and seven crashes, this eventful grand prix proved Irvine absolutely right. The Northern Ireland driver himself played a leading role in the spectacle.

The race coincided with a heatwave that, in combination with the circuit's long straights, threatened to be a hard test for brakes. The McLaren team were so concerned about potential brake problems that they even had new brake bells, to improve airflow, flown out on the night before the race.

Crash course

As the red lights went out, the leaders made a clean getaway, but there was mayhem towards the rear of the field. The Prost of Jarno Trulli went onto the grass while pushing up on the inside into Turn 1. It then slewed sideways and came back onto the track to take off Barrichello's Stewart and the Sauber of Alesi. Trulli and Alesi were out of the race. Barrichello limped on for another 14 laps before

Schumacher leads Hakkinen after exploiting his pole position to the full.

Jackie and Paul Stewart follow Herbert's progress into the points.

retiring. Both Barrichello and Alesi gave full vent to their frustrations, slamming Trulli for poor driving. Alesi was especially furious, as Trulli had clashed with him at the same place and time in last year's race.

Trulli defended himself by claiming that he had been forced to break when Frentzen had slowed suddenly.

Schuey's error

The final chicane at Turn 15 claimed the most spectacular scalps of the day. After BAR-Supertec driver Ricardo Zonta, the chicane brought no less than three former world champions to grief – Villeneuve, Hill, and race leader Michael Schumacher.

The German driver had started the race in a typically aggressive style, chopping across Hakkinen before the first corner, and forcing the Finnish driver to back off and fall into line. By lap 30, he had slowly eased away from Hakkinen, who let the Ferrari take a four-second lead. "I could have gone quicker in the first part of the race," Hakkinen commented, "but I saw no reason to. The risk was too high. It would have been so easy to make a mistake."

The mistake did duly happen, but it came not from Hakkinen but from Schumacher. Storming up to the final chicane on lap 33, the Ferrari driver came off the racing line, got on to some dust, and slammed sideways into the wall. This basic driver error totally transformed the race. The 10 points that Schumacher had in the bag were gifted to his McLaren-Mercedes rival.

Schumacher's own explanation of the incident was unburdened by any excessive modesty: "I usually make one mistake a year," the German driver said. "I hope this was the last."

Irvine fights back

Schumacher's exit gave Hakkinen a seven-second lead over Irvine, who battled with Coulthard to hold on to second position. On lap 40, Coulthard tried to go inside Irvine on the first corner, hoping to use the momentum on the start-finish straight to get past him. But the two cars touched and spun off. Although they got back on the track, they lost position. While Irvine began fighting his way up the field, Coulthard went into the pits for a time penalty, which effectively put him out of the points reckoning.

Making his way forward from eighth place, Irvine was a man on a mission. He got past Herbert's Stewart on lap 54 with a heart-stopping move that had both cars clipping the grass.

Disaster for Frentzen

Irvine got faster and faster, putting in a superb sequence of seven laps under 1 minute 21 seconds in a desperate attempt to close on the top three of Hakkinen, Frentzen, and Fisichella. Four laps from the finish, disaster struck Frentzen's Jordan. The car's right-front brake disc disintegrated and Frentzen crashed heavily into the tyre wall, suffering multiple injuries. It was a bitter blow for Jordan, who seemed certain of second place.

Hakkinen cruised to the flag, followed by Fisichella and Irvine. Afterwards, the Finn said: "Before today, I'd only scored two points at this circuit... Now I love Canada!"

Trulli's right rear wheel flies over Alesi's Sauber at the first curve.

Safety First

The 1999 Canadian Grand Prix will go down in the record books as the first in which the safety car led the way to the finish. The Mercedes CLK, driven by James Gavin, was called upon four times in all and drove a total of 14 laps.

James Gavin attracted a lot of attention because of his prominent role at Montreal. He commented: "There is a lot of pressure, because if anything goes wrong it will be down to me." A frustrated racer, who has just restarted his career in Formula 3000, Gavin would be happy to exchange the uprated 5.5 litre V-8 Mercedes for a smaller, lighter Formula One car. As he said: "None of the things that happen in a grand prix weekend will be a surprise, so being the safety car driver gives me excellent experience."

Keeping it going

The idea of using a safety car has come from oval racing in the United States. Formerly, any serious shunt would lead to a restart, which irritated drivers and spectators alike. Now, the safety car keeps the race going, with the bonus for spectators of bunching up the drivers ready for a rolling restart. As the Canadian Grand Prix showed, the result is better entertainment.

The safety car, a Mercedes CLK, leads the pack around the Circuit Gilles Villeneuve after one of many crashes in an accident-prone grand prix.

BETWEEN THE RACES

14 June BMW triumph at Le Mans

The annual Le Mans 24-hour classic has been won by a BMW sports car driven by Pierluigi Martini, Yannick Dalmas, and Joachim Winkelhoch. The car was designed and built at the factory at Grove in Oxfordshire where the new Williams-BMW Formula One car is being developed for the 2000 grand prix season. Despite the Le Mans victory, BMW motor sports director Gerhard Berger hinted that the company might withdraw from sports car racing next year in order to focus on Formula One.

The 24-hour race was marked by a spectacular accident involving a Mercedes CLK driven by Scottish driver Peter Dumbreck. The car flew into the air and somersaulted five times before crashing over a safety barrier into waste ground. Dumbreck, who fortunately avoided serious injury, said the crash "just came out of the blue".

16 June Hill bows out of F1

Former world champion Damon Hill has announced that he will retire from Formula One racing at the end of the current season. He said that the decision came "after much reflection".

Crashing out in the Canadian Grand Prix appears to have been the last straw for Hill, who has suffered a disappointing season, consistently outclassed by his team-mate Heinz-Harald Frentzen. Hill won his world championship in 1996, after being runner-up to Michael Schumacher in 1994 and 1995. He has struggled ever since being sacked by Williams at the end of his championship year. Last season he recorded an unexpected victory in the Belgian Grand Prix, but this failed to relaunch his career.

Hill is known to want to spend more time with his wife and four children. He has been critical of the present style of Formula One car, which he finds it no pleasure to drive, and of the amount of testing drivers are currently required to carry out, which leaves them with much less free time than previously.

As Hill is now 38 years old, the announcement of his retirement is hardly a surprise. Looking back, the driver said: "I am very proud of my record. Formula One has afforded me many incredible opportunities and I will cherish some fantastic memories."

The **BMW sports car** that won the Le Mans 24-hour race, photographed during the nighttime stage of the competition.

22 June Jenkins signs with Prost

Former Stewart designer Alan Jenkins is to become the new technical director of Prost. Jenkins had held discussions with Benetton and Sauber before taking up the Prost offer. He was replaced as technical director of Stewart this season by Gary Anderson.

24 June Next year's race calendar

The FIA has sprung some surprises in its provisional 2000 grand prix calendar. The first race of the season is to be held at the Sepang circuit in Malaysia — a decision that is unlikely to please the Australians, who are used to staging the opening grand prix. The season is set to finish earlier, with the final race at Suzuka shifted to early October.

Provisional race calendar for the year 2000 Formula One season

Date	Race	Circuit
20 February	Malaysian GP	Sepang
05 March	Australian GP	Melbourne
19 March	Brazilian GP	São Paulo
09 April	San Marino GP	Imola
23 April	Spanish GP	Barcelona
07 May	French GP	Magny-Cours
21 May	European GP	Nürburgring
04 June	Monaco GP	Monaco
18 June	Canadian GP	Montreal
02 July	British GP	Silverstone
16 July	Austrian GP	Spielburg
30 July	German GP	Hockenheim
13 August	Hungarian GP	Budapest
27 August	Belgian GP	Spa
10 September	Italian GP	Monza
24 September	U.S. GP	Indianapolis
08 October	Japanese GP	Suzuka

Jordan driver **Damon Hill** will soon be taking off his helmet for the last time.

25 June Eddie Jordan says Irvine is not for him

Eddie Jordan has quashed rumours that Eddie Irvine is set to rejoin the Jordan team next season as a replacement for the departing Damon Hill. Jordan said that Irvine "would be better off not coming back here, and it would be better for us if he didn't come back either".

Jordan's advice to Irvine is that he should stay at Ferrari. However, Irvine seems almost certain to move on. He told journalists recently: "I didn't come into Formula One to help Michael [Schumacher] win races."

25 June ITV at loggerheads with Ecclestone

ITV has been forced at the last minute to abandon plans to show live coverage of qualifying for the French Grand Prix, because this is apparently outside the terms of its contract to broadcast the sport.

This is the latest twist in a mounting confrontation between terrestrial television networks and Bernie Ecclestone, who is promoting his own digital TV service. The networks have in particular complained about being restricted to on-board camera coverage from a single car, while Ecclestone has cameras on every car in the grand prix.

Ecclestone was not available to comment on the controversy, as he is recovering from a heart-bypass operation at a London hospital.

Dressing for safety, not for style

THE FORMULA ONE DRIVERS of the 1950s, such as Ascari, Fangio, and Moss, raced in polo shirts and simple leather helmets. Sartorial stylishness was considered more important than safety, and many drivers paid with their lives. The biggest danger facing drivers then was fire from the poorly protected fuel tanks.

During the 1960s efforts were made to improve safety in all areas, which included protective clothing for the drivers. Over the intervening years, driver racewear has been transformed, designed not only to improve safety but to make driving a little less uncomfortable.

Head start

Particular attention has been paid to helmet design. If any cracks are spotted on the surface of a helmet, then it is immediately discarded. Drivers usually go through between six and 15 helmets in a season.

The FIA insists on full-face helmets with as small a facial aperture as possible. The Lexan visors that drivers wear are designed to withstand stone chips travelling at up to 500 km/h (310 mph), and are coated with

Graham Hill, Formula One champ during the 1960s, sports helmet, goggles, and trademark moustache.

several tear-off strips that the driver removes whenever his vision is impaired by oils, insects, or other track-borne debris.

Within the modern helmet there are special attachments for a radio microphone and earpieces (for communication with the pits), as well

as small vents for a drinks tube (water is essential to prevent dehydration inside the cars) and a medical air bottle (in the event of an accident).

Finned helmets

The smooth outline of the helmet aids the overall aerodynamic shape of the all-important driver-car combination, although many Formula One drivers are now using small fins at the back and sides of the helmet to reduce buffeting at high speeds. Padded neck supports are also used by

some drivers to increase comfort on high-speed corners when g-forces are at their greatest.

The driver is kitted-out from head to toe in flame-proof clothing made from Nomex. A lightweight synthetic material, it is designed to protect a person for 12 seconds in a 700°C hydrocarbon blaze, sufficient time for a driver to leap from his car to safety.

Nomex underwear consists of a full T-shirt and long johns, plus socks and a balaclava. Over this the driver wears Nomex overalls and flame-retardant boots and gloves.

A few of Michael Schumacher's extensive collection of helmets, complete with sponsors' logos.

David Coulthard models the latest in Nomex underwear.

Nomex gloves, overalls, and balaclava help protect Mika Hakkinen.

French Grand Prix

The weather at Magny-Cours was responsible for one of the most exciting races of recent years. The onset of rain during qualifying had produced a back-to-front grid; and with many of the best cars far down the order, mass overtaking was almost inevitable. Cars swept past each other, the lead changing a total of eight times during the race. Apart from the thrills and spills on the track, the conditions forced the teams and drivers to think out the most appropriate strategy for the race. But with the weather constantly alternating between wet and dry, the best-laid plans of many ended up in the gravel trap. Finally, Frentzen was let in to gain Jordan's first win of the season.

A torrential downpour at Magny-Cours triggered urgent pit-stops and the arrival of the safety car.

Track length 4.247 km (2.639 miles)
Race distance 305.806 km (190.024 miles) — 72 laps
1998 winner Michael Schumacher, Ferrari
Lap record 1:17.070 min, Nigel Mansell, Williams-Renault, 1992

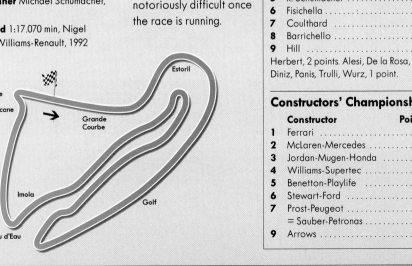

The Circuit

The Circuit de Nevers lies between Paris and Lyons and is home ground for the Prost-Peugeot team. Recently resurfaced, the track is smooth and lacks grip, a significant factor in the 1999 grand prix. The circuit challenges drivers with a tricky combination of high- and slow-speed corners, and overtaking is notoriously difficult once the race is running.

Race Result

	Driver	Time
1	Frentzen	1:58.24.343
2	Hakkinen	1:58.35.435
3	Barrichello	1:59.07.775
4	R. Schumacher	1:59.09.818
5	M. Schumacher	1:59.12.224
6	Irvine	1:59.13.244

Drivers' Championship

	Driver	Points
1	Hakkinen	40
2	M. Schumacher	32
3	Irvine	26
4	Frentzen	23
5	R. Schumacher	15
6	Fisichella	13
7	Coulthard	12
8	Barrichello	10
9	Hill	3

Herbert, 2 points. Alesi, De la Rosa, Diniz, Panis, Trulli, Wurz, 1 point.

Constructors' Championship

	Constructor	Points
1	Ferrari	58
2	McLaren-Mercedes	52
3	Jordan-Mugen-Honda	26
4	Williams-Supertec	15
5	Benetton-Playlife	14
6	Stewart-Ford	12
7	Prost-Peugeot	2
	= Sauber-Petronas	2
9	Arrows	1

Frentzen foremost as heavens open

Qualification

The normal practice for top Formula One teams during qualifying is to await events in their garages, only venturing out onto the track in the second third of the hour-long session. At Magny-Cours the weather caught them out. It had rained in the morning and the track was still wet, but most teams were sure that the track would dry during qualifying.

Weather aware

Stewart, Sauber, and Prost thought otherwise, and their drivers went out to complete an early quick lap in case the weather deteriorated. They were proved correct, as the rain began to fall with increasing intensity during the second half of the session. By then Barrichello, Alesi, and Prost had put in good laps that would see them on the front of the grid on Sunday.

Wet dunces

The rest of the field then came out in a desperate attempt to gain decent grid positions. The best of the late-comers were Coulthard and Frentzen, who handled the slippery conditions with great skill, managing fourth and fifth positions respectively. Michael Schumacher, an acknowledged rain specialist, took only sixth place, but Eddie Irvine, his Ferrari number two, managed only 17th position.

Qualifying Times

1	Barrichello	Stewart-Ford	1:38.441
2	Alesi	Sauber-Petronas	1:38.881
3	Panis	Prost-Peugeot	1:40.400
4	Coulthard	McLaren-Mercedes	1:40.403
5	Frentzen	Jordan-Mugen-Honda	1:40.690
6	M. Schumacher	Ferrari	1:41.127
7	Fisichella	Benetton-Playlife	1:41.825
8	Trulli	Prost-Peugeot	1:42.096
9	Herbert	Stewart-Ford	1:42.199
10	Zonta	BAR-Supertec	1:42.228
11	Diniz	Sauber-Petronas	1:42.942
12	Villeneuve	BAR-Supertec	1:43.748
13	Wurz	Benetton-Playlife	1:44.319
14	Hakkinen	McLaren-Mercedes	1:44.368
15	Zanardi	Williams-Supertec	1:44.912
16	R. Schumacher	Williams-Supertec	1:45.189
17	Irvine	Ferrari	1:45.218
18	Hill	Jordan-Mugen-Honda	1:45.334
19	Gené	Minardi-Ford	1:46.324
20	Badoer	Minardi-Ford	1:46.784
21	De la Rosa	Arrows	1:48.215
22	Takagi	Arrows	1:48.322

Mika Hakkinen gave a master class in overtaking – in the dry and wet – but he was unable to hold the lead in the face of Jordan's cunning single-stop strategy. Eddie Jordan's team read the weather best, and brought Heinz-Harald Frentzen home under the chequered flag.

The grid had a unfamiliar look. On pole was Rubens Barrichello, with Jean Alesi's Sauber alongside and the Prost of Olivier Panis a place back. Although McLaren's David Coulthard was on the second row, his team-mate was way back in 14th place, unknown territory for the usually front-row Finn.

But once the race got under way, the old order began to reassert itself. Coulthard charged to the front, deftly overtaking Alesi and Barrichello before opening up an impressive lead.

Struck by gremlins

The race belonged to him until the McLaren gremlins did their worst. "Things were looking good but then I had some sort of electrical failure," said Coulthard. "The engine turned itself off and that was that." His race was over by lap 10, leaving Barrichello to take over the lead. As ever, the Scotsman took the defeat manfully on the chin, but it was another blow in what was becoming a painful season. Further back, Mika Hakkinen began

Above: Barrichello's Steward-Ford leads out the field, thanks to gaining pole position in qualification.

Right: Heinz-Harald Frentzen zips his Jordan car past the flag to gain Eddie Jordan his first 1999 F1 win.

to storm his way to the front. In the space of just 10 laps he went from 14th position to fourth. In the process, he overtook Michael Schumacher at the end of the straight leading to the Adelaide hairpin – always a satisfying manoeuvre. Unknown at the time, Schumacher was running his car on a wet-weather set-up, and at this point in the race, when it was still dry, he was suffering accordingly.

And then the deluge

The threat of rain had been ever present throughout the day, and on lap 22 the weather took hold in earnest as the heavens opened. This was the signal for pit-stops en masse, as the cars came in for refuelling and wet-weather tyres. The rainfall increased in intensity, and the line between difficult and impossible racing began to be crossed. The safety car finally came out on lap 25, and for the next 10 laps tried to hold the cars on the circuit. Alesi was already off, however, and even with the safety car's presence, Villeneuve, Wurz, and Gené spun off in the torrential rain.

The rain had come to the aid of Michael Schumacher, whose wet-car set-up gave him an edge over his rivals. Although the rain had abated by lap 44, Schuey was able to slip past Barrichello to take the lead, and given his past performances in the wet, he looked good for another win. But the water was a treacherous helpmate, as moisture in the air began to interfere with the Ferrari's electrics, preventing Schumacher from communicating with the pits and, more seriously, only allowing him to engage first and second gear for a section of the race. The German driver made an early second pit-stop, but it failed to fully

Right: Electrical failure ended Coulthard's race at Magny-Cours.

solve his electrical problems and he was overtaken by the other leaders.

After a spin on the sodden lap 37, which set him back several places, Hakkinen once again worked his way up the field. He stayed out as long as possible before making his second pit-stop, and although Barrichello and

Frentzen were close by, McLaren were fairly sure that their driver had victory in the bag.

But unknown to the other teams, Jordan had decided as far back as lap 22, during the first round of stops, to fill Frentzen's large fuel tank with enough fuel to get him to the end.

Crucial to their reckoning was the knowledge that the heavy rain would slow down speeds, and also fuel consumption, making such a strategy feasible. Hakkinen and Barrichello pitted on lap 65, only to see Frentzen sail by, driving to the finish line to take his first victory for Jordan.

BETWEEN THE RACES

28 June *Jordan weather man holds key to win in France*

The Jordan team has revealed that during the French Grand Prix they employed one of their staff members to head upwind a few kilometres from the circuit and relay weather information to them via his mobile phone. Their one-man meteorological office forewarned them that monsoon-like rain was on its way to the course. Jordan's resultant pit strategy was crucial in ensuring victory for Heinz-Harald Frentzen. Knowing that heavy rain would be likely to bring out the safety car for an extended period, Jordan were able to modify their standard two-stop pit strategy to a single stop, calculating that Frentzen would have just enough fuel.

28 June *Schumacher blasts rear-light offenders*

Michael Schumacher is berating four of his fellow drivers for not using their rear warning lights during the French Grand Prix. "What's the point of discussing improving visibility in the rain if you don't enforce it?" Schumacher railed after the race. The guilty men were race-winner Heinz-Harald Frentzen, Mika Hakkinen, Rubens Barrichello, and Jarno Trulli.

Somewhat strangely, while all cars must be equipped with operational tail lights, there is no requirement in the rules for the drivers to have them turned on.

28 June *BAR-star slams Reynard for absences*

BAR's Jacques Villeneuve is clearly stating his objections to the repeated absences of technical director Adrian Reynard from the team. "We've hardly ever seen him," complains Villeneuve. "Adrian has got a lot of experience that would have been useful." One of the problems facing the beleaguered BAR team has been the different priorities of

effectiveness of car rear wings, making cars and tyres wider, replacing grooved tyres with slicks, thickening brake discs (to prevent catastrophic brake failures of the sort suffered by Frentzen in Canada), standardizing track-side kerb heights, and building asphalt run-off areas in place of gravel traps. The drivers hope that these ideas will be influential when the FIA and team bosses meet later this year to debate the F1 regulations.

7 July *Frentzen pledges future with Jordan for 2000*

The Jordan team is delighted with the progress made by Heinz-Harald Frentzen this season, and have announced their decision to exercise their option on the driver's contract for next year. Frentzen is also pleased with his relationship with the team, saying: "Together, we have shown that we are a force to be reckoned with, and I look forward to continuing the challenge for greater results in the year 2000."

7 July *F1 may quit Europe over EU restrictions*

The long-running dispute between the European Union and the FIA is flaring up again. Bernie Ecclestone has announced that several European GPs could be axed in favour of new venues in South America and Asia. The EU claims that anti-competition rules are being flouted by the FIA, and acting competitions commissioner Karel van Miert is threatening the FIA with the possible imposition of "substantial fines". Among the many charges levelled at the FIA are that it blocks rival racing organizations such as the US Indy Car league from racing in Europe, that it monopolizes TV rights, and that it prevents proper competition by tying teams and other organizations to restrictive contracts. The FIA refutes these charges.

The row is obstructing Ecclestone's planned flotation of his Formula One holding company on the stock market, a project in which he has sunk much of his time and resources. But also, Ecclestone and the FIA are attracted by the looser regulations that exist outside Europe, especially regarding tobacco advertising, and see new commercial opportunities opening up in what has become a genuinely global sport.

The failure of four drivers to turn on their tail lights at Magny-Cours earned them the wrath of Michael Schumacher.

BAR technical director Adrian Reynard: his absences have irked members of the team.

its team members. Villeneuve has grown used to the hands-on approach of his former Williams technical chief Patrick Head, while Reynard has commitments to other companies outside of BAR. It seems likely that Reynard will adopt an increasingly minor role in team matters.

1 July *Drivers offer their ideas for next season*

The Grand Prix Drivers Association is drawing up a list of proposals for F1 president Max Mosley to consider in the light of growing disquiet over racing regulations. In general, they are keen to reduce aerodynamic downforce in favour of better mechanical grip. Their proposals include reducing the

Contenders for the German crown

THE DOMINANCE OF MICHAEL Schumacher in the world of Formula One has tended to overshadow the contribution of other German drivers to the sport. Until the 1990s, German drivers had been few and far between in Formula One, but now Michael has been joined by younger brother Ralf and former rival, both on and off the track, Heinz-Harald Frentzen. And they are about to be joined by Nick Heidfeld, whose exploits in Formula 3000 are certain to provide him with an F1 seat for the next season.

Flourishing at Jordan

Since moving to Jordan at the end of last season, Frentzen has been a revelation. When he first moved to Williams he had the best car in Formula One, but apart from his single victory at Imola he was not a success. As team-mate Jacques Villeneuve's star rose, so that of Frentzen declined. But Jordan provides an atmosphere much more conducive to the development of his talents, and after the forbidding Williams duo of Patrick Head and Frank Williams he has easily adapted to Eddie Jordan, with his more relaxed approach to racing. As a consequence, Frentzen's confidence in his abilities has grown, translating itself into regular podium places.

Above: Heinz-Harald Frentzen, ascending star of the Jordan team.

Right: Nick Heidfeld, winner of round six of the 1999 F3000 at the A1-Ring in Spielberg.

Right: Ralf Schumacher has plenty of time to match his brother Michael's outstanding achievements.

Another reason for Frentzen's success may lie in the car set-ups for this season. He seems to thrive on the twitchy cars dictated by the latest safety regulations, with their four-grooved, low-grip tyres. Most drivers, including Jordan team-mate Damon Hill, don't like the new cars, but Frentzen, unlike Hill, has registered no complaints about his 1999 Jordan. The fact that he did so well in the slippery race conditions at Magny-Cours tends to support this theory.

Ralf finds his stride

Whereas Frentzen likes it at Jordan, Ralf Schumacher seemingly did not, and in contrast to Frentzen he has got on well at his new Williams home after leaving Jordan last year. But when he first came onto the scene as Michael's kid brother, Schuey Junior had a lot to live up to. Perhaps this was a reason why he tried a bit too hard, racing too fast, crashing too often, taking off an embarrassingly large number of drivers in the process, including his illustrious elder brother.

While at Jordan last year, Ralf Schumacher began to grow up as a grand prix driver, and since moving to Williams this growing maturity has seen him deliver some impressive performances on the track. The car is clearly underpowered, but with improving aerodynamics and the prospect of a new BMW engine for next season, the future looks good for Schumacher at Williams.

Hungry for glory

Germany has a double world champion in Michael Schumacher, but with the emergence of Frentzen and Ralf Schumacher as drivers of note there is now strength in depth. And with the addition of Nick Heidfeld, there could be four Germans racing next season. The question remains whether these new drivers have the ability and luck to join Schuey Senior and win the title. Only time will tell, but there is no doubt that each one will be keen to break Schuey's grip on the crown.

British Grand Prix

Since the introduction of safety measures to the track layout, Silverstone has lost some of its old reputation for exciting racing. But this year's race began with a major event, as Schumacher sped off the tarmac and smashed into the tyre wall at Stowe. Not only did Schuey's crash transform the race, it would transform the whole season ahead. With Schumacher injured, and Coulthard winning at Silverstone, it seemed that McLaren would have an easy run to the world championship. But the German driver's absence also opened up new possibilities for his number two, Eddie Irvine.

Medical and safety personnel attend Michael Schumacher after he hit the tyre wall.

The Circuit

Well-liked for its enthusiastic home fans, the track at Silverstone remains one of the most demanding in Formula One. Chicanes were constructed on many bends, but the fast corners on this track always promise spectacular racing.

Silverstone

Track length 5.137 km (3.192 miles)
Race distance 308.221 km (191.525 miles) — 60 laps
1998 winner Michael Schumacher, Ferrari
Lap record 1:24.475 min, Michael Schumacher, Ferrari, 1997

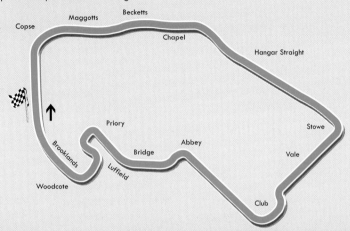

Becketts
Maggotts
Copse
Chapel
Hangar Straight
Stowe
Priory
Abbey
Vale
Bridge
Brooklands
Luffield
Club
Woodcote

Race Result

	Driver	Time
1	Coulthard	1:32.30.144
2	Irvine	1:32.31.973
3	R. Schumacher	1:32.57.555
4	Frentzen	1:32.57.933
5	Hill	1:33.08.750
6	Diniz	1:33.23.787

Drivers' Championship

	Driver	Points
1	Hakkinen	40
2	M. Schumacher	32
=	Irvine	32
4	Frentzen	26
5	Coulthard	22
6	R. Schumacher	19
7	Fisichella	13
8	Barrichello	10
9	Hill	5
10	Herbert, Diniz	2
11	De la Rosa, Panis, Alesi, Wurz, Trulli	1

Constructors' Championship

	Constructor	Points
1	Ferrari	64
2	McLaren-Mercedes	62
3	Jordan-Mugen-Honda	31
4	Williams-Supertec	19
5	Benetton-Playlife	14
6	Stewart-Ford	12
7	Sauber-Petronas	3
8	Prost-Peugeot	2
9	Arrows	1

Schumacher's loss leads to British gains

Qualification

At Silverstone, Mika Hakkinen gained his sixth pole from eight races. Michael Schumacher had driven what seemed to be a definitive lap, putting down a time nearly a full second ahead of Irvine and Barrichello. But out came Hakkinen and chopped three-tenths off the Ferrari number one's qualifying time. Rising track temperatures then made Hakkinen's position unassailable.

Hill is set for glory

An alternating silver-red-silver-red line-up of McLarens and Ferraris occupied the front of the grid. The Jordans filled the next two slots; Frentzen's fifth place was no surprise, but Hill in sixth showed new determination to do well in front of the home crowd for the last time. Hill said that his performance owed much to an improved gearbox and a better overall set-up of his Jordan 199.

Benetton cover the back

Behind the leading six, Barrichello drove his Stewart to seventh, Ralf Schumacher took his Williams to eighth, and Villeneuve did well to get his BAR to ninth. The stop-start season for Benetton continued in negative mode; both cars were relegated to the nether regions, with Fisichella in 17th and Wurz one place behind. The Arrows and Minardis took last positions.

Qualifying Times

1	Hakkinen	McLaren-Mercedes	1:24.804
2	M Schumacher	Ferrari	1:25.223
3	Coulthard	McLaren-Mercedes	1:25.594
4	Irvine	Ferrari	1:25.677
5	Frentzen	Jordan-Mugen-Honda	1:25.991
6	Hill	Jordan-Mugen-Honda	1:26.099
7	Barrichello	Stewart-Ford	1:26.194
8	R Schumacher	Williams-Supertec	1:26.438
9	Villeneuve	BAR-Supertec	1:26.719
10	Alesi	Sauber-Petronas	1:26.761
11	Herbert	Stewart-Ford	1:26.873
12	Diniz	Sauber-Petronas	1:27.196
13	Zanardi	Williams-Supertec	1:27.223
14	Trulli	Prost-Peugeot	1:27.227
15	Panis	Prost-Peugeot	1:27.543
16	Zonta	BAR-Supertec	1:27.699
17	Fisichella	Benetton-Playlife	1:27.857
18	Wurz	Benetton-Playlife	1:28.010
19	Takagi	Arrows	1:28.037
20	De la Rosa	Arrows	1:28.148
21	Badoer	Minardi-Ford	1:28.695
22	Gené	Minardi-Ford	1:28.772

If Silverstone signalled the death knell for Michael Schumacher's world championship hopes, it was a good race for British spectators, with three UK drivers in the top six. David Coulthard collected maximum points, managing to hold off a spirited challenge from Eddie Irvine, while Damon Hill came an impressive fifth in his last home grand prix.

The lights went out and the 1999 British Grand Prix got underway. But not for long: Zanardi stalled on the grid and Villeneuve's gearbox packed up. Waving red flags and radio messages to the drivers signalled a restart, but Schumacher did not register them. Trying to make up ground after being overtaken by Coulthard and Irvine, his rear brakes suddenly failed and he tore into a tyre wall, breaking his leg. A plume of smoke from his front tyres underlined his untimely exit from the race.

At the restart, the field got away cleanly. Hakkinen drove through Copse well in the lead, although his team-mate lost the opening battle to Irvine; Coulthard had to content himself with following the Ferrari at a distance and waiting for the first

Mika Hakkinen congratulates his exultant team-mate David Coulthard on his storming win at Silverstone.

round of pit-stops to offer a chance of gaining an advantage.

Behind the three lead drivers, Frentzen was in fourth place, closely followed by Ralf Schumacher, who was leading Hill, Barrichello, Alesi, Herbert, and Diniz.

Coulthard gains the edge

David Coulthard pitted first on lap 24, spending just 7.6 seconds stationary before racing back up the pit lane. Frentzen and Ralf Schumacher followed, but adjustment to the Jordan driver's wing allowed Schuey Junior to exit ahead of Frentzen – a lead he would keep to the end of the race. Irvine came in on lap 26 but overshot

his mark – partially unsighted by Hakkinen's McLaren – and took a full 12 seconds before being released by the "lollipop" man. Irvine was to rejoin the track behind Coulthard.

Mika Hakkinen was comfortably in the lead when he pitted in lap 26, but then mechanics had problems with his McLaren's left rear wheel. Unhappy with the wheel, Hakkinen soon came in for a second stop. After a protracted 27 seconds all seemed well and Hakkinen raced away to set the fastest lap of the day. But this was

Below: Following the restart, and Schumachers's disastrous departure, Hakkinen leads Irvine past Copse.

Above: Hakkinen's car finally loses the defective left rear wheel that effectively cost him the race.

merely a prelude to disaster: his car and left rear wheel parted company on lap 29. Hakkinen limped back to receive a new wheel, but Ron Dennis ended his race after a few more laps.

From then on the pattern of the Grand Prix was set, confirmed by the second set of pit-stops. Coulthard raced over the line to the chequered flag, followed by Irvine and Ralf Schumacher. The Jordan drivers Frentzen and Hill were fourth and fifth respectively, while Diniz took the last point for Sauber. After being cruelly thwarted by mechanical failure in France, David Coulthard richly deserved his win at Silverstone.

Brake failure leads to Schumacher shunt

Michael Schumacher's shattered Ferrari, its front wheels bundled unceremoniously into the cockpit, is lifted from the track onto a recovery vehicle.

Thundering down Hangar Straight, Schumacher was determined to get past Irvine after a bad start had set him back from second to fourth place. Braking late in an attempt to squeeze past Irvine, his rear brakes suddenly failed and he shot across the gravel trap to hit an unbelted tyre wall at 67 mph (107 km/h). The gravel trap had taken some speed off the Ferrari, but not enough — Schumacher had broken both the tibia and fibula bones in his right leg. He was taken to the nearby Northampton General Hospital where he underwent basic surgery to set the fractures.

BETWEEN THE RACES

12 July Ecclestone refutes drug rumours

Bernie Ecclestone denies that there is any truth to allegations in Britain's Sunday Times that drug smuggling is rife in Formula One. The newspaper report suggests that hard drugs have been smuggled between South America and Europe using F1 cargo containers. Ecclestone retorts: "The Sunday Times are getting into the tabloid way and sensationalizing things. If they had anything that was true they could have printed it last week or next week. Strange they picked the day of the British Grand Prix."

12 July Irvine requests parity with Schumacher

Even before Michael Schumacher's accident in the British Grand Prix yesterday, Eddie Irvine has been pressing for equal status in the Ferrari team next year. Offers to race with the Stewart team have strengthened Irvine's hand, but it is well known that Schumacher expects the Ferrari team to be built around him. If Irvine is unable to persuade Ferrari to accept his terms, then it seems unlikely that he will race for the Italian team next season.

12 July Resigning Mosley's plans for F1

Max Mosley has announced that he will stand down from his post as president of the FIA by 2001. Discussing the future of Formula One, he said that the sport would have to abandon its reliance on sponsorship from tobacco companies. The cut-off point will be 2006, when the European Union imposes its blanket ban on tobacco advertising, but Mosley believes that the sport should gradually wind down its commercial relationship with the tobacco industry.

Mosley has confirmed that narrow, grooved tyres will stay until at least the end of next season, rejecting driver claims that they make overtaking more difficult. However, the FIA president accepts that aerodynamic improvements might be causing a problem for the sport, and suggests that F1 engineers should come up with a solution to minimize aerodynamic grip.

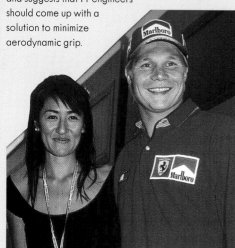

Mika Salo, seen with wife Noriko, will drive for Ferrari until Schumacher returns.

13 July Salo to fill Schuey's seat

Ferrari has announced that Finnish driver Mika Salo will replace Michael Schumacher until the German driver has recovered from the injuries he sustained at Silverstone. Salo has been released from his contract with BAR, where he acted as a reserve driver, and he is set to act as Eddie Irvine's number two at the forthcoming Austrian Grand Prix.

14 July Hill to carry on at Jordan

The extended procrastination that has attended Damon Hill's decision over his future in Formula One seems finally to have been ended by his confirmed intention to continue racing until the end of the season. His decision to stay on was welcomed by Heinz-Harald Frentzen, who said: "I could not imagine a better team-mate to secure a third place in the constructor's championship for Jordan. If Damon is fully motivated, he is still a hell of a racing driver." Team owner Eddie Jordan now faces the task of finding Hill's replacement for the next season.

22 July Will General Motors enter F1?

General Motors, the world's largest automobile manufacturer, are considering whether to make an entry into the world of Formula One in the near future. Herb Fischel, GM's Executive Director of Motorsports, refuses to be drawn on the issue but admits that his company has a strong interest in Formula One, and would be keen to promote its image on a global stage. But Fischel warns that if GM were to make a commitment to F1, they would need to have a guarantee that regulations within the sport would remain stable.

24 July McLaren driver line-up seems certain for 2000

Mercedes-McLaren will now run with Mika Hakkinen and David Coulthard during next season. That Hakkinen would race with McLaren has been virtually certain for some time, but doubts have arisen over fellow driver David Coulthard. A poor showing in early races, combined with an inability to get past back markers, has earned him some criticism, but his good result at Silverstone and his second place on the grid at Austria have won him friends at Mercedes-McLaren. Coulthard has been in talks with Ron Dennis and Norbert Haug, and while he admits that nothing has been signed he has said: "I have no reason to think anything other than that we will be back together again next year."

Mercedes' Norbert Haug (left) and Ron Dennis will maintain their drivers for 2000.

Keeping Formula One safety on track

Tests have proved that tyre barriers still deserve their place in Formula One.

Safety measures of all kinds are given the utmost importance in Formula One, and while there are many accidents in the sport, serious injury and death are rare. In the past this was far from the case, but since the 1970s the number of racing fatalities has progressively decreased. During the 1960s, 27 drivers were killed in Formula One; in the 1970s this figure had decreased to 12; in the 1980s it was seven; and so far during the 1990s only two have died – Roland Ratzenberger and Ayrton Senna, both killed at the 1994 San Marino Grand Prix. The deaths of Ratzenberger and Senna have, in turn, acted as a stimulus for further safety improvements.

In essence, track safety is based upon slowing down the speed of a car when it leaves the track, and reducing the force of the impact when the car hits a barrier. In the 1960s heyday of drivers like Jim Clark and Graham Hill, the racing circuit was full of potentially fatal obstacles, such as trees and concrete barriers. These have been removed and replaced by flat run-off areas to allow the driver to reduce speed in a controlled way.

Gravel traps

Designed to radically slow the pace of a spinning car, gravel traps are situated around major bends. In this role they are highly effective, but when a car runs onto a gravel trap in a straight line, the level of deceleration is markedly less. The role of gravel traps has become a controversial issue in Formula One, especially after Michael Schumacher's accident at Silverstone. Many drivers and racing pundits believe other measures should be adopted, although FIA research shows that gravel traps slow all vehicles, whether spinning or running in line. The opponents of gravel traps suggest several options, including a more extensive use of tarmac run-off

Left: Armco barriers such as these at Monte Carlo offer some "give" on collision, improving driver safety.

areas and banked gravel traps that slope upwards towards the tyre barriers. While such measures are expensive, circuit organizers at Monza are introducing a number of raised gravel traps in readiness for this year's Italian Grand Prix.

Armcos and tyre walls

Supplementing gravel traps and run-off areas are the barriers that separate drivers from spectators. Armcos are simple metal barriers which deform on impact and – as long as the impact is not at 90 degrees – allow the car to "slide" along the barrier, absorbing energy in the process.

More effective for dealing with full-on collisions are tyre walls. Despite their "low-tech" appearance they have been found to be highly effective in halting a speeding car with the minimum of driver injury. What is debated is whether they should be belted (held together by rubber conveyor sheets or belts) or unbelted. Schumacher hit a wall of unbelted tyres, and it is possible that a belted tyre barrier would have reduced the car's penetration and offered Schuey greater protection.

Yet thanks to modern trackside safety, Schuey escaped with a broken leg; 30 years ago, the accident would probably have been fatal.

Below: Formula One is a rich sport and its professional medical staff receive state-of-the-art equipment.

Austrian Grand Prix

The Austrian Grand Prix marked the start of Life after Schumacher. Eddie Irvine claimed he could take over the reins at Ferrari, but doubters saw the title going to McLaren by default. After the McLaren drivers managed to shoot themselves in the foot during the opening lap at the A1-Ring, Irvine convincingly answered his critics with his second victory of the season. Once again, the race strategy adopted by Ferrari was virtually faultless, and Irvine proved that he could race under pressure. Even Michael Schumacher had to admit that the Irishman had driven a fine race.

The Ferrari team salute Eddie Irvine as he beats David Coulthard to the chequered flag.

The Circuit

The A-1 Ring was built during the winter of 1995–96 to replace the Osterreichring track, scene of 18 grand prix races. Like its predecessor, the A1-Ring encourages exhilarating, high-speed racing, its long sweeping corners providing excellent opportunities for cars and drivers to demonstrate their qualities. On the minus side, overtaking may be inhibited.

A1-Ring

Track length 4.319 km
(2.684 miles)
Race distance 306.640 km
(190.543 miles) — 71 laps
1998 winner Mika Hakkinen, McLaren-Mercedes
Lap record 1:11.814 min, Jacques Villeneuve, Williams-Renault, 1997

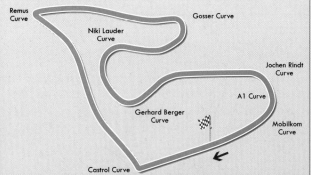

Remus Curve
Niki Lauder Curve
Gosser Curve
Jochen Rindt Curve
A1 Curve
Gerhard Berger Curve
Mobilkom Curve
Castrol Curve

Race Result

	Driver	Time
1	Irvine	1:28.12.438
2	Coulthard	1:28.12.751
3	Hakkinen	1:28.34.720
4	Frentzen	1:29.05.241
5	Wurz	1:29.18.796
6	Diniz	1:29.23.371

Drivers' Championship

	Driver	Points
1	Hakkinen	44
2	Irvine	42
3	M. Schumacher	32
4	Frentzen	29
5	Coulthard	28
6	R. Schumacher	19
7	Fisichella	13
8	Barrichello	10

Hill, 5 pts. Diniz, Wurz, 3 pts. Herbert, 2 pts. Alesi, De la Rosa, Panis, Trulli, 1 pt

Constructors' Championship

	Constructor	Points
1	Ferrari	74
2	McLaren-Mercedes	72
3	Jordan-Mugen-Honda	34
4	Williams-Supertec	19
5	Benetton-Playlife	16
6	Stewart-Ford	12
7	Sauber-Petronas	4
8	Prost-Peugeot	2
9	Arrows	1

Irvine romps home as McLaren falter

Qualification

The surprise of the qualifying session was the performance of both Stewarts: Rubens Barrichello claimed fifth and Johnny Herbert was just a tenth slower in sixth. The team put this down to engine modifications and a new electronic differential. Sadly, for Stewart, accidents and reliability problems would prevent any race exploitation of their good results.

McLaren mastery

David Coulthard, who had been strong in the warm-up sessions, thought he was at the front of the grid, but a brilliant lap by Hakkinen pushed him back a place and gave the Finnish driver his seventh pole position of the season. Once again, Hakkinen had proved himself the master of the single flying lap. The domination of McLaren in qualifying was particularly worrying for Ferrari, as Irvine was nearly a full second down on Hakkinen.

Spilt-second timing

Of the others, Heinz-Harald Frentzen confirmed the now general belief that he and Jordan are a coming force in Formula One, securing a good fourth place. Ferrari new boy Mika Salo did well to scrape into seventh place, literally a thousandth of a second ahead of Ralf Schumacher's Williams.

Qualifying Times

1	Hakkinen	McLaren-Mercedes	1:10.954
2	Coulthard	McLaren-Mercedes	1:11.153
3	Irvine	Ferrari	1:11.973
4	Frentzen	Jordan-Mugen-Honda	1:12.266
5	Barrichello	Stewart-Ford	1:12.342
6	Herbert	Stewart-Ford	1:12.488
7	Salo	Ferrari	1:12.514
8	R. Schumacher	Williams-Supertec	1:12.515
9	Villeneuve	BAR-Supertec	1:12.833
10	Wurz	Benetton-Playlife	1:12.850
11	Hill	Jordan-Mugen-Honda	1:12.901
12	Fisichella	Benetton-Playlife	1:12.924
13	Trulli	Prost-Peugeot	1:12.999
14	Zanardi	Williams-Supertec	1:13.101
15	Zonta	BAR-Supertec	1:13.172
16	Diniz	Sauber-Petronas	1:13.223
17	Alesi	Sauber-Petronas	1:13.226
18	Panis	Prost-Peugeot	1:13.457
19	Badoer	Minardi-Ford	1:13.606
20	Takagi	Arrows	1:13.641
21	De la Rosa	Arrows	1:14.139
22	Gené	Minardi-Ford	1:14.363

Above: Spun round by David Coulthard, Mika Hakkinen (nearer car) is left pointing the wrong way. Left: Hakkinen prays for deliverance.

If the chequered flag went to Irvine, Hakkinen deserved a special prize. An error by David Coulthard sent him from first to last place, but the Finn refused to surrender. In a sustained display of controlled, aggressive driving he fought his way back through the field to win a place on the podium. The four points he won were enough to keep him ahead of Irvine, with all still to play for.

Disaster stuck Mika Hakkinen on just the second corner of the race, the tight uphill right-hander called the Remus Kurve. Both McLarens had got away cleanly from the start, with Hakkinen taking the lead. At Remus, Hakkinen drove a little too wide. Coulthard thought he had a chance and tried to squeeze through on the inside, but in the process nudged his team-mate into a spin.

Neither car was damaged and the McLaren number two maintained his lead. Hakkinen had the indignity of seeing 21 cars drive past him before he could resume his own race. Meanwhile, Coulthard was stricken: "It was my nightmare scenario, taking my team-mate off in the first lap." But there was a race to be won, and he began to build his lead ahead of the pack. Things were looking good for Coulthard until just before his single pit-stop on lap 39. He had been held up by Zanardi, who cut his lead to just under eight seconds, before he sped into the pit-lane for a mediocre 10.5-second stop. The other leaders also began to peel into the pits with the notable exception of Eddie Irvine.

Above: Eddie Irvine shows his heels through the final laps at Spielberg.

The Ferrari driver stayed out and with a clear track ahead of him began a series of flying laps that Schumacher would have been proud of.

Coulthard had failed to make up ground since leaving the pits and was falling back behind Irvine when the new Ferrari number one finally pitted on lap 44. An excellent 8.6 seconds stationary was enough to get Irvine out again ahead of Coulthard. It was not looking like McLaren's day.

Meanwhile, Hakkinen drove one of the races of his life in an attempt to reverse his misfortune. If nothing else, on that day Hakkinen proved conclusively that overtaking is possible in Formula One, as he moved from 22nd to 3rd place in just 40 laps. Although most of the cars ahead of Hakkinen were in no way comparable to the McLaren, the Finnish driver executed a fine passing manoeuvre against Heinz-Harald Frentzen's Jordan at the end of lap 33, and by the finish had closed to only 20 seconds or so behind the two leading drivers, Coulthard and Irvine.

Duel for the crown

During the final few laps Irvine had to fight hard to prevent Coulthard getting past him, especially when his brakes began to fade. "When I eased off to save the brakes," the Ferrari driver said after the race, "Coulthard caught me quicker than I expected and I had to push hard and forget about everything else. The chequered flag couldn't come soon enough, but I proved I can do the job."

Above: Mika Salo, replacement Ferrari number two, took ninth place.

*Right:
Victory could
not be sweeter for
Eddie Irvine in his
first outing as number
one driver for Ferrari.*

BETWEEN THE RACES

Test-driver status did not secure Luca Badoer the number two slot at Ferrari following Schuey's accident.

26 July Badoer says he should be the new Ferrari driver

The Italian Ferrari test driver Luca Badoer was unable to hide his disappointment when he learned the news that the number two slot at Ferrari had been allocated to Mika Salo. Badoer, who also drives for Minardi, complained: "I'm very disappointed with that decision. I do not agree with it because I think I was the right person. I'm under contract for that job." Replying to those who said that he would have difficulty surviving the pressure sure to be placed upon him by the Italian media, he said: "I have a very strong character and mind. I know I could have coped with the pressure. But I have to accept the decision." Badoer refused to be drawn when asked whether he would continue to drive for Minardi next season.

26 July Coulthard apologizes to Hakkinen after Austrian GP

McLaren are playing down differences between Mika Hakkinen and David Coulthard arising from their collision during the Austrian Grand Prix. The drivers had conspicuously retired to the McLaren motor home to discuss the incident immediately following the race. Emerging from there, Coulthard accepted full responsibility for the accident: "It was my fault. I messed up. I'm sorry. If I could change it, I would." In his turn, Hakkinen was conciliatory: "I was very upset, but I have calmed down now. David did not mean to do that; it was not on purpose. It is something we have to learn from."

26 July Lauda and Berger criticize Benetton car

The veteran Formula One racers Niki Lauda and Gerhard Berger are not impressed by the car supplied by Benetton to their fellow Austrian driver Alexander Wurz. Lauda is particularly hard on Benetton. "If you design a bullshit car," he has said, "you can't do anything in a season. If it is bad at the start, you are stuck with it all season."

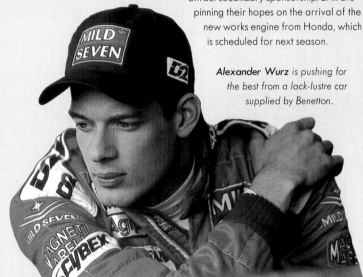

Alexander Wurz is pushing for the best from a lack-lustre car supplied by Benetton.

Berger, who raced with the Benetton team in 1996 and 1997, lays the blame at the door of chief designer Nick Wirth: "[He] has designed three Benettons now and none of them have been very good." Nevertheless, Wurz was able to finish in fifth place during the race at the A-1 Ring, a significant improvement on his generally poor form this season.

26 July Brembo brakes check

Following Michael Schumacher's accident in the British Grand Prix, the brake manufacturer Brembo has introduced a warning system for drivers. If the hydraulic brakes undergo a massive drop in pressure, a warning light will flash in the cockpit alerting the driver to the problem. In addition to Ferrari, Jordan, Benetton, Prost, Sauber, and Minardi all tested the system during the Austrian Grand Prix.

27 July Pollock denies sacking rumour

Craig Pollock, the head of British American Racing, has rejected rumours that he might face the axe as a result of his team's poor performance this season. Admittedly only in its first year of racing, BAR has still failed to produce a car that could be called reliable, making life virtually impossible for its drivers. British American Tobacco, who bankroll BAR, have given their support to Pollock but they are concerned at a budget overspend thought to be around £20 million, and also by the team's failure to attract secondary sponsorship. BAR are pinning their hopes on the arrival of the new works engine from Honda, which is scheduled for next season.

29 July Van Miert goes as EU apologizes to FIA

EU competitions commissioner Karel van Miert is being replaced by Mario Monti, who is thought to have a more open attitude towards Formula One. Van Miert had been accused by FIA President Max Mosley of leaking confidential documents to the press and acting in a manner that "was not appropriate for somebody who occupied a quasi-judicial position."

The FIA is engaged in a lawsuit with the EU, and has issued a writ stating that the actions of the EU have "caused the loss of revenue to the FIA and tarnished the reputation of the FIA as a respectable and efficiently run organization". The EU has admitted that certain confidential documents were distributed to journalists, and has published a statement expressing regret for issuing statements "which have been understood as prejudicing issues relating to the FIA".

The Prost-Peugeot relationship seems set to come asunder.

30 July Prost may end deal with Peugeot

The struggling Prost team's relationship with Peugeot is on rocky ground. Peugeot's two seasons with Prost have been less successful for the French engine manufacturer than earlier ones with McLaren and Jordan. A Peugeot spokesman said: "We have a contract until 2000 and we are still in discussion." However, Peugeot want to develop their interest in the World Rally series, and resources are likely to be diverted away from their commitment to Formula One.

Dreams and reality: the season to date

THE AUSTRIAN GRAND PRIX marked the beginning of the second half of the 1999 season. How had the teams fared so far, and what were their hopes for the rest of the year?

As in previous seasons, the points table was divided into three broad sections. At the top, and surprising nobody, were McLaren and Ferrari, preoccupied in their struggle for the world championships for driver and constructor. Further down was the mid-table battle, fought by Jordan, Williams, Benetton, and Stewart. The Jordan team had emerged as the "best of the rest", and looked set to achieve their pre-announced objective for the season, namely to take third place in the constructor's championship. The Williams car driven by Ralf Schumacher lacked power but was still consistently picking up points, a tribute to the driver and the car's nicely calculated aerodynamics and general reliability. By contrast, the Benettons and Stewarts lacked any consistency: occasionally they raced very well, more often they were a disaster.

At the bottom of the table were Sauber, Prost, Arrows, Minardi, and BAR – all performing poorly. More had been expected of Sauber and, especially, Prost, and cracks were beginning to appear in both of those teams. Minardi acknowledged that they participated in Formula One mainly to make up the numbers, and the recent financial upheavals at Arrows had forced a similar outlook on the team fronted by Nigerian Prince Malik.

Poor performance by Sauber is reflected in Jean Alesi's uneasy expression.

BAR: smoke but no fire?

The most surprising and lamentable performance of the season so far had come from British American Racing. As a new team in Formula One, no observer had expected regular podium placings, but given the team's resources and the proven track record of its personnel, BAR's total lack of reliability remained a mystery.

Alongside Minardi, BAR was the only team not to have picked up a point.

The future? By half-way, the basic shape of the season is usually defined and dramatic surprises are rare. Accordingly, the top two teams will continue to slug it out for the title, the middle four will be fighting their own battle, and the bottom five will gain points only when others slip.

Former world champion Jacques Villeneuve will be hard pressed to rescue BAR from an ignominious first season.

Arrows will need several large slices of good luck to make an impression on the championship.

German Grand Prix

In one of the stranger races of the season, McLaren seemed set to dominate following good qualifying performances. But in the event Ferrari scored an amazing one-two to get maximum points. Mika Salo's performance was little less than extraordinary. Recently drafted in to fill Michael Schumacher's seat, he shot away at the start, held off Coulthard like an old professional, and would have won the race if he hadn't been obliged to let Eddie Irvine through. Embarrassed by the nature of his win, the former number two gave Salo his victory trophy.

Ferrari team policy dictated that Eddie Irvine should take the laurels at Hockenheim.

The Circuit

The Hockenheim Ring is one of the longest grand prix circuits. In the main it comprises a series of fast straights and corners, but there is a slower stadium complex of tight corners before the finishing line. Setting up cars for both of these track sections is difficult because the downforce needed for the tight bends also slows the cars on the straights.

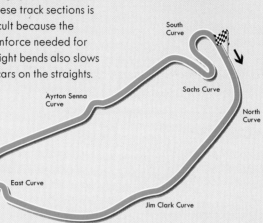

Hockenheim

South Curve

Sachs Curve

North Curve

Ayrton Senna Curve

East Curve

Jim Clark Curve

Track length 6.822 km (4.239 miles)
Race distance 307.014 km (190.775 miles) — 45 laps
1998 winner Mika Hakkinen, McLaren-Mercedes
Lap record 1:46.211 min, David Coulthard, Williams-Renault, 1994

Race Result

	Driver	Time
1	Irvine	1:21:58.594
2	Salo	1:21:59.601
3	Frentzen	1:22:03.789
4	R. Schumacher	1:22:11.403
5	Coulthard	1:22:15.417
6	Panis	1:22:28.473

Drivers' Championship

	Driver	Points
1	Irvine	52
2	Hakkinen	44
3	Frentzen	33
4	M. Schumacher	32
5	Coulthard	30
6	R. Schumacher	22
7	Fisichella	13
8	Barrichello	10
9	Salo	6

Hill, 5 pts. Wurz, Diniz, 3 pts. Herbert, Panis, 2 pts. De la Rosa, Alesi, Trulli, 1 pt.

Constructors' Championship

	Constructor	Points
1	Ferrari	90
2	McLaren-Mercedes	74
3	Jordan-Mugen-Honda	38
4	Williams-Supertec	22
5	Benetton-Playlife	16
6	Stewart-Ford	12
7	Sauber-Petronas	4

Prost-Peugeot, 3 pts. Arrows, 1 pt.

Agony for McLaren, ecstasy for Ferrari

Qualification

Eddie Irvine had a poor time during qualifying, plagued by brake problems and, in his last flying lap, slow traffic. He was fifth on the grid, just out of touch with the leaders and, perhaps more significantly, a place behind Mika Salo, who had run a superb session in the still-unfamiliar Ferrari.

McLaren century

In the 10th race of the season, Mika Hakkinen secured his eighth pole position (and McLaren's 100th overall). The Finnish driver's ability to squeeze everything out of both car and track was little less than phenomenal. David Coulthard would have joined him on the front row except for a brilliant lap by Heinz-Harald Frentzen, possibly inspired by Hockenheim's massed ranks of cheering German supporters.

Lower orders

Ralf Schumacher could not respond in like fashion, finding himself in 11th place alongside Villeneuve. The Prost team could take heart from a surprisingly good qualifying session, with Panis in seventh place and Trulli directly behind him in ninth. But Alain Prost's countryman Jean Alesi had the humiliation of starting the race on the back row of the grid, his session aborted by brake problems.

Qualifying Times

1	Hakkinen	McLaren-Mercedes	1:42.950
2	Frentzen	Jordan-Mugen-Honda	1:43.000
3	Coulthard	McLaren-Mercedes	1:43.288
4	Salo	Ferrari	1:43.577
5	Irvine	Ferrari	1:43.769
6	Barrichello	Stewart-Ford	1:43.938
7	Panis	Prost-Peugeot	1:43.979
8	Hill	Jordan-Mugen-Honda	1:44.001
9	Trulli	Prost-Peugeot	1:44.209
10	Fisichella	Benetton-Playlife	1:44.338
11	R. Schumacher	Williams-Supertec	1:44.468
12	Villeneuve	BAR-Supertec	1:44.508
13	Wurz	Benetton-Playlife	1:44.522
14	Zanardi	Williams-Supertec	1:45.034
15	Gené	Minardi-Ford	1:45.331
16	Diniz	Sauber-Petronas	1:45.335
17	Herbert	Stewart-Ford	1:45.454
18	Zonta	BAR-Supertec	1:45.460
19	Badoer	Minardi-Ford	1:45.917
20	De la Rosa	Arrows	1:45.935
21	Alesi	Sauber-Petronas	1:45.962
22	Takagi	Arrows	1:46.209

Mika Hakkinen's terrible run of luck showed no sign of letting up in Germany. For the third race in succession he was denied victory through no fault of his own. He might reasonably have expected to collect 30 points in total, but walked away with just four. At Silverstone it had been his left rear wheel parting company with the rest of the car; in Austria it had been an inadvertent nudge from his team-mate; while at Hockenheim it was a combination of a refuelling error followed by a spectacular blow-out.

After a good, clean start from pole position, Hakkinen began to open up a lead which he held comfortably until his pit-stop on lap 24. Frustratingly, the fuel nozzle refused to engage properly and Coulthard's rig was eventually used. The McLaren was forced to stand in the pits for 24 agonizing seconds. Back on the track, Hakkinen was now in fourth place.

The Finn then began a charge through the field, but while driving at full throttle down the last straight before the stadium complex his left rear tyre exploded. The McLaren conducted a series of violent spins which sent it across the grass, through a gravel trap, and then into a tyre wall.

Salo maintains his lead despite heavy pressure from Coulthard.

A Stewart passes Diniz as he spins out after colliding with Villeneuve.

The accident had shades of Michael Schumacher at Silverstone, but the car had slowed sufficiently for the Finn to emerge unhurt. Hakkinen could only walk back to the pits and wonder at his bad luck – world championships have turned on fewer points than he had lost over the last three races.

Salo seizes his chance

The start had been a dream for Mika Salo. He leapt from fourth to second, slipping past Coulthard and Frentzen. While Coulthard chased after Salo's Ferrari, Frentzen fell back to be overtaken by Rubens Barrichello, who was running a light fuel load, having opted for a two-stop strategy. Further

Irvine (right) could not quite match Salo's pleasure at their double win.

back, Villeneuve spectacularly crashed into Diniz, and both cars ended up stationary in the gravel trap. This was to be Villeneuve's tenth DNF (Did Not Finish) in 10 races.

Coulthard, meanwhile, was running hard behind Salo, but the Ferrari driver refused to be pressured into a mistake and held his line. On lap 10, Coulthard was forced to brake hard to avoid running into the back of Salo. The cars touched briefly; the Ferrari was unscathed but damage to the McLaren forced Coulthard to return to the pits for a new nose cone.

Mika Hakkinen ruefully surveys his McLaren after a burst tyre took him out of the race.

This was another embarrassment for Coulthard to enter into his race diary, and although he eventually fought his way back to a very creditable fifth position (and two points), the German Grand Prix was clearly destined to benefit his arch-rivals at Ferrari.

Self-sacrifice for Salo

After Hakkinen's refuelling mishap in the pits, Salo had the gratifying experience of leading a grand prix for the first time in his career. But Eddie Irvine overtook Frentzen and by lap 25 was behind his team-mate. Mindful of Ferrari's rule forbidding competition between Scuderia drivers, Salo obliged and let his senior through to take the lead. Irvine was then to encounter problems with his oil temperature, forcing him to drive a conservative race to the flag, with Salo following in close attendance.

Irvine steals ahead

A short distance behind the Ferraris were the two German drivers Frentzen and Ralf Schumacher, who had both driven solid if unspectacular races. For the spectators it was only limited consolation for not having Schuey Senior at their home grand prix. But the large Ferrari contingent could cheer on Eddie Irvine, who, with three wins this season, had stolen an eight-point lead over Hakkinen. McLaren could only hope that fortune would smile on them in Hungary.

BETWEEN THE RACES

2 August *Coulthard to keep parity with Hakkinen in 2000*

McLaren have revealed that David Coulthard will have equal status with Mika Hakkinen during the 2000 season. Martin Whitmarsh, managing director at McLaren, said: "David will start next season level with Mika, regardless of what happens this year. To prevent him racing would be wrong. We want the drivers doing the best job they can." Despite these comments from Whitmarsh, McLaren have the contractual right to ask a driver to support a team-mate, and if events develop into a straight McLaren-Ferrari fight towards the end of this season, it is possible that the team may wish to exercise that right.

2 August *Albert Park to start 2000 season*

Melbourne is now confirmed to be the venue for the opening grand prix of next year. When the provisional calendar for the 2000 season was published earlier this season, the FIA had selected Malaysia to host the opening race, followed by Melbourne.

David Coulthard will race for McLaren in 2000, says team principal Ron Dennis (left).

date in the new season, and asked for a change. The Melbourne Grand Prix is now rescheduled to take place on 12 March 2000.

2 August *Grooves and gravel traps are suspect, says Ecclestone*

Bernie Ecclestone has entered the current heated controversy over safety regulations by criticizing both grooved tyres and gravel traps. His comments go against the official line promoted by FIA president Max Mosley. Ecclestone is convinced that grooved tyres add to the dangers facing the driver. "To my mind," he has said, "you'd be better off with sticky tyres and cars that don't fly

years that gravel beds are quite useless. They do not brake the cars effectively. What we need is a run-off area with an extremely rough asphalt surface, and the track surface itself should be rougher, so that the cars don't slide so much."

2 August *Brake misunderstanding ended Hill's German GP*

After completing only 13 laps, Damon Hill retired from the German Grand Prix on the basis that his brakes were beginning to go off. Hill admitted that the team were not happy with his early retirement, but justified his action by saying: "I am in the cockpit and took the decision that it was not safe to carry on." After the race, however, Jordan technical director Mike Gascoyne said that there was nothing wrong with the brakes. The problem may have been that a new, harder type of brake pad had recently been installed in Hill's Jordan, and the English driver was not accustomed to it.

5 August *Stewart transmutes into Jaguar*

Britain's Autosport magazine has revealed that the Ford-owned Stewart Formula One team will be renamed Jaguar next season, and its number one driver will be Ferrari's Eddie Irvine. In a straight team swap, Stewart driver Rubens Barrichello will move over to Ferrari where he will partner Michael Schumacher.

Irvine has become increasingly dissatisfied at having to act as Schumacher's deputy, and now sees a new future within the huge Ford empire, which fully intends to mount a serious challenge for the world championship within the next two seasons. The motor giant also wants to increase brand awareness for its Jaguar operation on a global scale, and as a consequence the new car will be painted in British racing green. Ford president Jac Nasser says he hopes to emulate the way in which Ferrari have used their

success in Formula One to promote their image as a manufacturer.

The increasingly direct way in which Ford are intervening within the Stewart team raises questions concerning how the team is managed, and the position of Jackie Stewart and his son Paul. The Stewarts are keen to retain control of the team they built up over the last few years, but, after Ford's purchase of Stewart last June, the final say rests with the Ford management.

Rubens Barrichello will be trading places with Eddie Irvine next year, taking over as the Ferrari number two.

9 August *Are Formula One drivers suffering Repetitive Strain Injury?*

A Paris hospital has announced that of the 22 drivers tested after the French Grand Prix, 14 were suffering from the RSI-like symptoms of numbness, pain, and tingling in the fingers. The symptoms, which are more common in keyboard operators, are caused in F1 by vibrations transmitted by the steering wheel and gearshift paddles. FIA medical chief Sid Watkins is not unduly alarmed, however, considering the sensations to be little more than the muscular equivalent of blisters, with no likely long-term impact.

Melbourne's Albert Park is now reinstated as host to the opening F1 race in 2000.

But the Australians felt slighted by the decision and they complained to the FIA. Fortunately for the Australians, the Malaysian GP authorities were concerned about the short interval between their inaugural race on 17 October this year and the proposed

off the road. I never agreed with the idea of grooves. I said to Max that if eventually you add enough grooves, you'll end up with slicks."

On the subject of gravel traps, the Formula One boss has equally damning comments: "It has been my opinion for

Schumacher hits the sidelines

THE ACCIDENT SUFFERED BY Michael Schumacher at Silverstone was a personal disaster. He had been in touch with Hakkinen in the driver's table, and looked as likely as he ever would to bring the trophy of the world championship back to Ferrari. But the fractures to his right leg at Stowe shattered any chance of that happening in the 1999 season.

To make matters worse for the German driver, the points made available by Hakkinen's ensuing bad run of luck went not to him but to his team-mate, and thus arch-rival, Eddie Irvine. Watching Irvine on television as he collected the points in Austria and Germany must have been particularly galling for Schumacher. Although steadfastly declaring his support for the team, Schumacher certainly did not want to see the Ferrari number two walking away with the world championship he had worked nearly three years to acquire.

While anxiously waiting to see how the season would take shape, Schumacher had to put up with speculation among his Formula One acquaintances and the press concerning his future

with Ferrari. Why, everyone was asking, should the team pay him $25 million a year when Irvine seemed to be doing a perfectly good job for a fee roughly a fifth of the size?

Although Schumacher is the dominant driver of his age, Irvine has been steadily closing the ability gap and has staked a legitimate claim to equal status at Ferrari, or at any other team he chooses. Recuperating in his comfortable home in Switzerland, Schumacher must be aware that the old order is looking less certain.

Race or recuperation?

The date for Schumacher's return to Formula One has become one of the most debated topics of the season. Reams have been written about the many psychological factors that might now influence him and affect his driving, but according to Niki Lauda, who was nearly burnt to death at the Nurburgring in 1976 but

returned to racing within six weeks, he should get back on track as soon as possible. "A shunt like Michael's is nothing," says Lauda coolly. "He has broken a leg, no more."

A new game, a new pack

Michael Schumacher is renowned for his tough, focussed personality, and the chances of his being adversely affected by a relatively minor accident are extremely slim. The problem is essentially a tactical one. Despite protestations to the contrary, Schuey, like other forceful F1 drivers, races not for the team but for himself – he finds

the best team he can simply in order to realize that goal. The idea of acting as Eddie Irvine's number two will be hard – probably too hard – for the German ace to swallow.

In the nature of the sport, Formula One has itself progressed since Schumacher's accident. The focus of attention has shifted away from the fight between him and Hakkinen to that between Irvine and Hakkinen. No driver is bigger than the sport, and the F1 juggernaut rolls remorselessly onward. It was just bad luck for Michael Schumacher that he missed out this year.

Due to his accident, the presence of German national hero Michael Schumacher was necessarily in image only at the Hockenheim Ring.

Hungarian Grand Prix

It is said that the Hungaroring is Monaco minus the glamour. Overtaking on this narrow circuit ranges from the very difficult to the virtually impossible, making for fairly predictable races. Not that Mika Hakkinen was complaining. The nightmare of the previous three races was over, and he led from start to finish to collect maximum points. McLaren team-mate David Coulthard also did particularly well, managing to pressure Irvine into a points-losing mistake that gained him second place. The balance of power, held by Ferrari in Austria and Germany, had swung back to McLaren.

Winning at the Hungaroring signalled the end of a disastrous sequence of races for Mika Hakkinen.

The Circuit

Built in 1986 especially for grand prix racing, the Hungaroring is a relatively slow, bumpy, and slippery track. A good starting position and careful pit and race strategy tend to win races — only cars with a clear speed advantage can overtake successfully.

Track length 3.972 km (2.468 miles)
Race distance 305.836 km (190.043 miles) — 77 laps
1998 winner Michael Schumacher, Ferrari
Lap record 1:18.308 min, Nigel Mansell, Williams-Renault, 1992

Race Result

	Driver	Time
1	Hakkinen	1:46:23.536
2	Coulthard	1:46:33.242
3	Irvine	1:46:50.784
4	Frentzen	1:46:55.351
5	Barrichello	1:47.07.344
6	Hill	1:47.19.262

Drivers' Championship

	Driver	Points
1	Irvine	56
2	Hakkinen	54
3	Coulthard	36
	=Frentzen	36
5	M. Schumacher	32
6	R. Schumacher	22
7	Fisichella	13
8	Barrichello	12

Salo, Hill, 6 pts. Wurz, Diniz, 3 pts. Herbert, Panis, 2 pts. De la Rosa, Alesi, Trulli, 1 pt.

Constructors' Championship

	Constructor	Points
1	Ferrari	94
2	McLaren-Mercedes	90
3	Jordan-Mugen-Honda	42
4	Williams-Supertec	22
5	Benetton-Playlife	16
6	Stewart-Ford	14
7	Sauber-Petronas	4

Prost-Peugeot, 3 pts. Arrows, 1 pt.

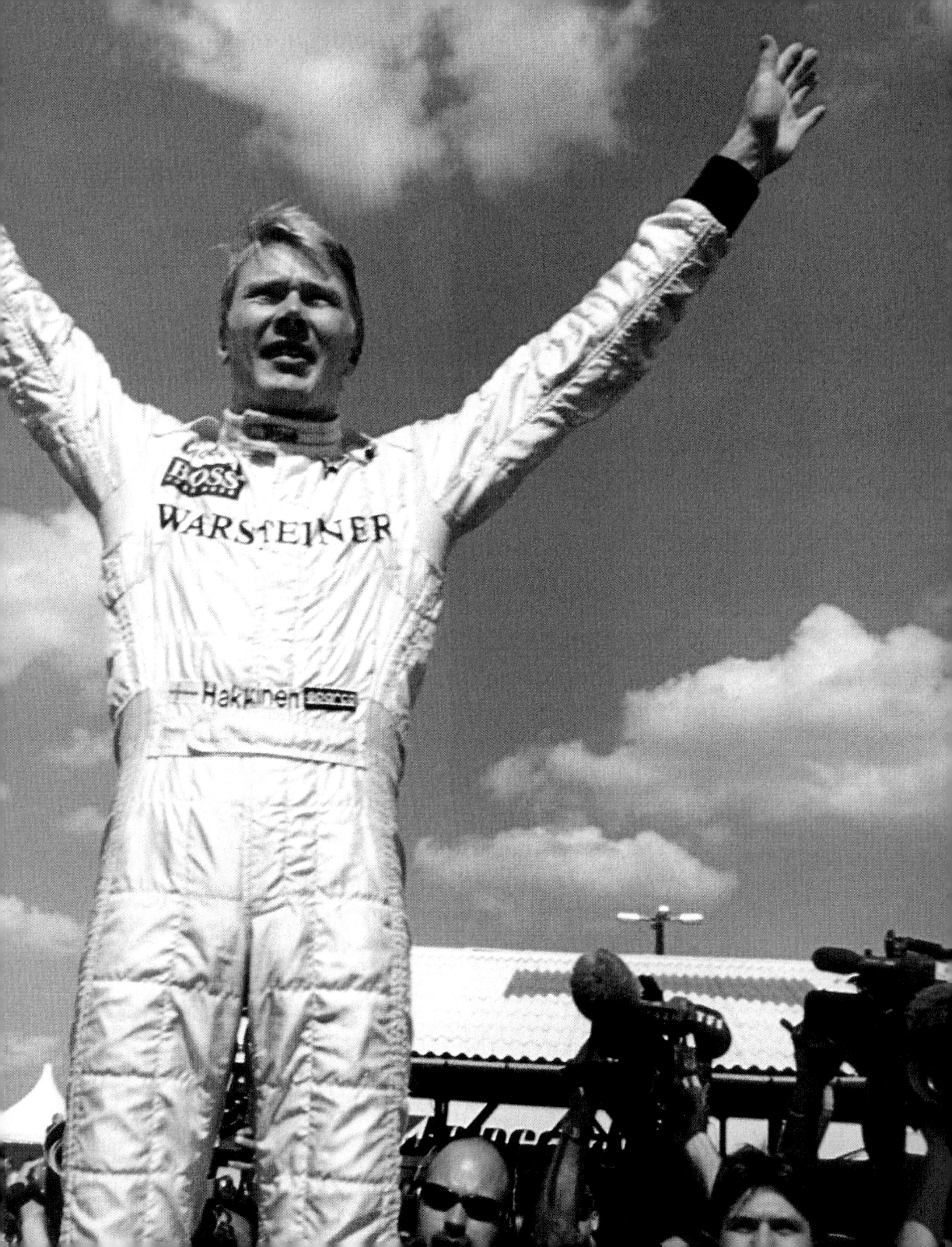
BOSS
WARSTEINER
Hakkinen

Silver Arrows on target in Hungary

Qualification

Confident after his victories in Austria and Germany, Eddie Irvine said he believed that the track in Hungary offered the best chance for his Ferrari to gain a pole position. He was nearly right, just beaten to first on the grid by Hakkinen, who tends to make pole something of a personal fiefdom. Coulthard was unable to top Irvine for speed, and became the bottom layer of a McLaren-Ferrari-McLaren sandwich.

Alarm for Ferrari

In the light of his Hockenheim successes, there was surprise and dismay in the Ferrari camp when Mika Salo only managed 18th. Something was wrong with the car set-up, but no one could quite put their finger on the problem.

Benetton revival?

Using Bridgestone's very soft tyre compound, Benetton's Fisichella gained fourth place alongside Coulthard. With Wurz in seventh, Benetton were well placed. The third row was yellow, filled by the Jordans of Frentzen and Hill. The Hungaroring seems to suit the Jordan car and the team were confident that points would fall their way. Williams, Jordan's only rival for third place in the championship, did surprisingly badly, with Zanardi in 15th out-qualifying the younger Schumacher by a place.

Qualifying Times

1	Hakkinen	McLaren-Mercedes	1:18.156
2	Irvine	Ferrari	1:18.263
3	Coulthard	McLaren-Mercedes	1:18.384
4	Fisichella	Benetton-Playlife	1:18.515
5	Frentzen	Jordan-Mugen-Honda	1:18.664
6	Hill	Jordan-Mugen-Honda	1:18.667
7	Wurz	Benetton-Playlife	1:18.733
8	Barrichello	Stewart-Ford	1:19.095
9	Villeneuve	BAR-Supertec	1:19.127
10	Herbert	Stewart-Ford	1:19.389
11	Alesi	Sauber-Petronas	1:19.390
12	Diniz	Sauber-Petronas	1:19.782
13	Trulli	Prost-Peugeot	1:19.788
14	Panis	Prost-Peugeot	1:19.841
15	Zanardi	Williams-Supertec	1:19.924
16	R Schumacher	Williams-Supertec	1:19.945
17	Zonta	BAR-Supertec	1:20.060
18	Salo	Ferrari	1:20.369
19	Badoer	Minardi-Ford	1:20.961
20	De la Rosa	Arrows	1:21.328
21	Takagi	Arrows	1:21.675
22	Gené	Minardi-Ford	1:21.867

Lacking a grand prix of their own, Finnish Formula One fans make a point of coming to the Hungaroring in a big way. No fewer than 23 extra flights had been booked from Finland to Hungary over the weekend, and the mass of blue-and-white flags testified to the intensity of their support for the Finnish drivers, Hakkinen and Salo. The fans were not to be disappointed as Hakkinen made a text-book demonstration of how to win a grand prix: he qualified superbly, started cleanly, and ran to the finish reliably. McLaren and the Finnish fans were well satisfied.

David Coulthard, who is usually very sprightly at a grand prix start, was left standing as Fisichella and Frentzen sailed by when the lights went out. But the Scot kept his head and drove one of his best races of the season. He set the fastest lap of the race, had the edge over Irvine, and had he got away better he might have threatened Hakkinen for the chequered flag.

Benetton's big chance

Fisichella's start – a "blinding" one according to Coulthard – saw him comfortably into third position. The run of poor performances lately gripping Benetton seemed to be over, but disaster struck just before the

Waving Finnish flags dominate the Hungarian skyline, outnumbering those of German Ferrari fans.

second series of pit-stops. The car suddenly lost power, fuel pressure began to fall, and when Fisichella went into the pits the engine died. The only crumb of comfort for Benetton came with a good seventh place for Wurz, but that was still one tantalizing place out of the points.

Irvine, who had got away well just behind Hakkinen, began to have serious tyre problems. Soon the silver McLaren of Coulthard was looming increasingly large in his rear mirrors. The moment of drama came soon

Seconds from the start, Fisichella's Benetton (right) lies third after Hakkinen and Irvine.

With Coulthard at his tail, Irvine found his Ferrari "jumping all over the road" due to defective tyres.

after the drivers pitted together, one behind the other. Irvine emerged from the pits still in the lead, but on lap 62 his Ferrari ran off the road and onto the grass verge. Irvine quickly regained control but by then he had lost track position to the McLaren. Coulthard slipped away, gaining nearly 17 seconds over Irvine by the end of the race. Irvine's team-mate Salo limped home into 12th place.

Jordan enjoyed their race, with both drivers gaining points. Frentzen's fourth place came as no surprise, but sixth position for Damon Hill marked something of a return to form – Hungary has always been a favourite hunting ground for the Englishman.

Clear of Irvine's Ferrari, Coulthard hurtles toward second place to complete a 16-point one-two for McLaren.

BETWEEN THE RACES

16 August Prost forced to continue with Peugeot

The Prost team's hopes of finding another engine supplier for next season seem to have been dashed. Supertec and Mugen-Honda were approached by Alain Prost but were unable to supply the French team. The present Prost-Peugeot contract runs until the end of 2000, when it is thought that Peugeot will pull out of Formula One altogether and concentrate their energies on rallying. For their final season in F1, Peugeot will supply Prost with a new, lighter A20 engine to replace this year's A18.

16 August Sylvester Stallone to promote F1 in US with new film

American film star Sylvester Stallone was spotted at the Hungarian Grand Prix making preparations for his forthcoming Formula One movie "Into Thin Air". Stallone has been a regular visitor at European grand prix races over the last couple of years, and is clearly fascinated by the sport. Bernie Ecclestone is keen to develop an interest in Formula One in the US, and it is hoped that the Stallone film will help raise the profile of the sport, which has a US Grand Prix scheduled for 2000.

Sylvester Stallone schmoozes with McLaren's Ron Dennis.

23 August Despite a brilliant test drive, Schumacher is out of Spa

Any chance of Michael Schumacher making an early return to racing has been prevented by renewed pain in his fractured leg. A superb display of driving by Schumacher at the Mugello track on Friday proved that

he had lost none of his skill and aggression, but his leg is not considered sufficiently strong to allow a comeback for the Belgian Grand Prix. Just 40 days after sustaining the injury at Silverstone, Schumacher climbed into the Ferrari and completed 65 fast laps of the Mugello circuit. By the end of the session, the German driver had lapped faster than his Ferrari team-mate Eddie Irvine and stand-in driver Mika Salo.

Ross Brawn, Ferrari's technical director, was not at all surprised by Schumacher's performance: "That's Michael. That's why he's so special. He is a racer, and he was always extremely keen to get back in the car and race." Although Schumacher felt only limited discomfort directly after the session, he experienced more pain after a cycle ride the following Monday, sufficient to rule him out of the next GP.

23 August Paul Ricard circuit ready to make a return

In an interview with the French newspaper Nice-Matin, FIA president Max Mosley said that the French Grand Prix would move from its present venue at Magny-Cours to the Paul Ricard circuit in the south of France. The Paul Ricard circuit has had a long history of hosting the French Grand Prix, but since 1991 Magny-Cours has been the race venue. The FIA's contract with Magny-Cours ends in 2002, and it seems likely that the race will then move to Paul Ricard.

26 August Brawn denies Todt is being levered out of Ferrari

Ferrari technical supremo Ross Brawn has emphatically denied that he is in any way involved in an attempt to oust sporting director Jean Todt from his position at Ferrari. The rumour caused Brawn considerable embarrassment, and he was quick to issue a rebuttal: "As far as I am concerned, there is no pressure for Jean to leave. If there is, it is certainly not coming from me. Ferrari would be much worse off without Jean. He is a pretty key figure, and I am sure if he

Jarno Trulli will join Jordan in 2000, following Damon Hill's retirement from F1.

Nick Heidfeld, F3000 world champion in 1999, is joining Prost next season.

wasn't here, we wouldn't be achieving what we are." Todt also rejected any idea that he might be preparing to leave the Italian F1 team.

27 August "Musical chairs" for 2000 almost over

The signing of Formula 3000 star Nick Heidfeld to the Prost team for the 2000 season signals the beginning of the final stage of the annual chase for a drive in Formula One. Alongside Heidfeld at Prost will be Jean Alesi, who will have left Sauber (Alesi's place there will be taken by Mika Salo). Of this year's Prost driver line-up, Trulli will depart for Jordan to replace retiring Damon Hill, while Panis's future looks uncertain but may include a drive for Arrows or Minardi. Higher up the table, McLaren,

Williams, and Benetton are keeping their drivers, while Ferrari have made a direct swap with Stewart, exchanging Irvine for Barrichello.

28 August New gravel traps for Italian Grand Prix

In the wake of Michael Schumacher's accident at the British Grand Prix, gravel traps at the Monza circuit have been modified so that they slope upwards from the track towards the barrier. Tests have shown that these upward-sloping traps are more effective in slowing a car's progress. The new gravel traps have been positioned at what are potentially the most dangerous corners of the Monza circuit: the first chicane, the second Lesmo bend, Ascari, and Parabolica.

Fitter drivers for faster cars

DRIVING A FORMULA ONE CAR around a track might not seem a particularly strenuous activity to the casual observer. In reality, the highest levels of physical and mental fitness are essential for success. And as the performance of cars has increased, so have the demands on the driver. For example, the strains of acceleration and deceleration in the car can be literally breathtaking; it is worth remembering that an F1 car can accelerate to 100 mph (160 km/h) and then brake to a standstill in a little over six seconds.

High-speed bends

The most intense g-forces are created by cornering at high speeds. At 2-g the driver's weight is effectively double that of normal, and at some bends the lateral force is rated at above 3.5-g. On some extreme corners, the driver's peripheral vision is lost because blood flow to the eyes is temporarily impaired.

Apart from having to withstand kinetic stresses, dehydration is a constant problem. It is not unusual for a driver to lose a litre of body fluid during a race, a loss greater than that experienced by a top-class tennis player during a similar time span.

Fitter drivers

Formula One drivers have always tended to be fairly robust individuals, but only in the last few years has physical fitness been taken to the high levels now standard in the sport. In the past, drivers would collapse with heat exhaustion after a race; this would be a rarity amongst today's superset drivers, such as Michael Schumacher and David Coulthard. Formula One drivers spend several hours a day in the gym improving and maintaining their general fitness and developing the physical resources essential for successful driving. An F1 driver needs to exert a force of around 20 kg (44 lb) to turn a steering wheel at speed, and special machines have been developed to assist them in strengthening their arms. Again, the neck muscles of drivers are subjected to severely punishing g-forces during cornering, and drivers are provided with work-out machines dedicated to strengthening that vulnerable area. Typical of the modern generation of Formula One drivers is Benetton's

F1 drivers such as David Coulthard are advised by members of dedicated human performance teams.

Exhausted, Britain's Nigel Mansell is helped from the track. Training today better prepares drivers for the rigorous demands of F1 racing.

Alexander Wurz, who is also a keen rock climber and former mountain bike champion. In addition to a long work-out in the gym, he jogs for up to an hour and cycles for at least two hours a day. Wurz and his team-mate Giancarlo Fisichella have the benefit of a superbly equipped new human performance centre, managed by ex-Marine Bernie Shrosbee.

F1 drivers need tremendous concentration, especially when they are fatigued. Bernie Shrosbee leaves nothing to chance: "I can get one of the drivers off the bike or the rower knowing that they are near to physical exhaustion and then make them carry out reaction skills. This is very important because it gets the brain, the neurological system, and the muscles working together." And as every trainer now knows, physical and mental fitness are key elements in winning the championship.

Recorded as being the heaviest driver at the start of the 1999 season, Alexander Wurz cycles to control his weight as well as build stamina.

Belgian Grand Prix

Driving with great assertion, David Coulthard came first at Spa and effectively announced himself as a title contender alongside Hakkinen and Irvine. After the race, a surly Hakkinen felt Coulthard had robbed him of maximum points when the two McLarens touched while vying for the lead at the first corner, La Source. But most observers thought that Hakkinen was the more blameworthy driver. The incident was a dramatic demonstration of the price McLaren must occasionally pay for their "two drivers racing" policy. They also face the danger of points won being shared too evenly between their drivers, letting Ferrari through to seize the championship.

The two McLarens touch at La Source corner, Mika Hakkinen driving on the inside.

Track length 6.968 km (4.330 miles)
Race distance 306.597 km
(190.516 miles) — 44 laps
1998 winner Damon Hill, Jordan-
Mugen-Honda
Lap record 1:51.095 min,
Alain Prost, Williams-
Renault, 1993

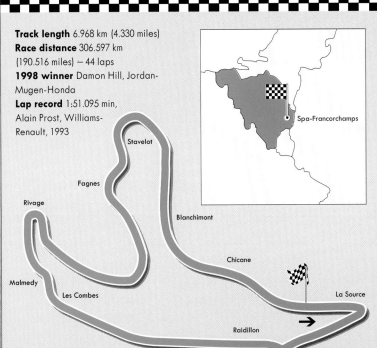

Spa-Francorchamps

The Circuit

Following the route of an old country road through the wooded hills of the Ardennes, the Spa-Francorchamps circuit is the longest in F1. Interestingly combining high-and low-speed sections, the course includes a very fast bend at Blanchimont and the fast and demanding downhill bend at Eau Rouge.

Race Result

	Driver	Time
1	Coulthard	1:25.43.057
2	Hakkinen	1:25.53.526
3	Frentzen	1:26.16.490
4	Irvine	1:26.28.005
5	R. Schumacher	1:26.31.124
6	Hill	1:26.37.973

Drivers' Championship

	Driver	Points
1	Hakkinen	60
2	Irvine	59
3	Coulthard	46
4	Frentzen	40
5	M. Schumacher	32
6	R. Schumacher	24
7	Fisichella	13

Barrichello, 12 pts. Hill, 7 pts. Salo, 6 pts.
Wurz, Diniz, 3 pts. Herbert, Panis, 2 pts.
De la Rosa, Alesi, Trulli, 1 pt.

Constructors' Championship

	Constructor	Points
1	McLaren-Mercedes	106
2	Ferrari	97
3	Jordan-Mugen-Honda	47
4	Williams-Supertec	24
5	Benetton-Playlife	16
6	Stewart-Ford	14
7	Sauber-Petronas	4

Prost-Peugeot, 3 pts. Arrows, 1 pt.

McLaren surge ahead of Ferrari

Qualification

Eau Rouge, arguably the most testing corner in Formula One, claimed two more victims during qualifying, when both BAR cars crashed heavily. Villeneuve and Zonta were running too low a ride height and bottomed out

Jacques Villeneuve's BAR smashes into the belted tyres at the top of Eau Rouge.

when coming out of the corner and going up the hill. Both drivers were unhurt, although the team had to work heroically to get two cars on the grid for the following day's racing.

McLaren mastery

Out at the front, both McLarens were the best part of a second ahead of the two Jordans on the second row. Mika Hakkinen's delight at gaining his 10th pole of the season was increased by the knowledge that his chief rival Eddie Irvine was in sixth place. Williams could be satisfied, with Ralf Schumacher in fifth and an improving Zanardi in eighth.

Qualifying Times

1 Hakkinen	McLaren-Mercedes	1:50.329
2 Coulthard	McLaren-Mercedes	1:50.484
3 Frentzen	Jordan-Mugen-Honda	1:51.332
4 Hill	Jordan-Mugen-Honda	1:51.372
5 R. Schumacher	Williams-Supertec	1:51.414
6 Irvine	Ferrari	1:51.895
7 Barrichello	Stewart-Ford	1:51.974
8 Zanardi	Williams-Supertec	1:52.014
9 Salo	Ferrari	1:52.124
10 Herbert	Stewart-Ford	1:52.164
11 Villeneuve	BAR-Supertec	1:52.235
12 Trulli	Prost-Peugeot	1:52.644
13 Fisichella	Benetton-Playlife	1:52.782
14 Zonta	BAR-Supertec	1:52.840
15 Wurz	Benetton-Playlife	1:52.847
16 Alesi	Sauber-Petronas	1:52.921
17 Panis	Prost-Peugeot	1:53.148
18 Diniz	Sauber-Petronas	1:53.778
19 Takagi	Arrows	1:54.099
20 Badoer	Minardi-Ford	1:54.197
21 Gené	Minardi-Ford	1:54.557
22 De la Rosa	Arrows	1:54.579

Coulthard, flanked by Frentzen (right) and his less-than-pleased team-mate Hakkinen, enjoys his victory.

Despite the bad feeling following the McLarens' battle for the first corner, the Spa race ended in another McLaren one-two win, pushing the team to the lead in the constructors' championship. The Ferraris were not on the pace in Belgium and their lack of speed and poor set-up caused much heart-searching, with Di Montezemolo openly criticizing his engineers. Criticism was also directed at Ferrari from outside the team, when Salo was seen to block Ralf Schumacher as he was closing on Eddie Irvine.

After poor starts in the last two races, Coulthard shot away from the grid at Spa. Hakkinen had problems before the lights went out. "When the red lights start to show," Hakkinen later explained, "you want to feel the clutch, to know where it is, and it grabbed very quickly. The car moved forward very slightly, but then I immediately stopped completely and put the clutch back in. As I did that, of course, the lights went out."

As they drove towards the tight hairpin of La Source, Coulthard was slightly in the lead and cut across the apex to defend his line. Hakkinen, on the inside, had nowhere to go and there was a slight coming together. Coulthard immediately moved over, and neither car was damaged as they exited from the corner with Coulthard in the lead. Hakkinen did not chase, uncertain over his car and seemingly shaken by the experience. He was lucky not to get a stop-go penalty for jumping the start, although loss of the lead was probably the most just punishment in this case.

Coulthard speeds ahead of both the field and his team-mate Hakkinen.

Just ahead of Gené's Minardi, Villeneuve would at last succeed in completing a grand prix in a BAR-Supertec.

Ferrari were clearly not competitive when compared with the McLarens, but Eddie Irvine made a good start and jumped two places to fourth, some distance behind Heinz-Harald Frentzen. Irvine seemed set to finish in this position and gain three still vital championship points. But it then emerged that Williams had a single pit-stop strategy rather than the double one of most other teams. After his single pit-stop, Ralf Schumacher looked good to get past Irvine when the Irishman made his second stop.

Salo blocks Schumacher

The Ferrari team instructed Mika Salo, then in front of Schumacher, to slow his pace and block the Williams driver, gaining Irvine sufficient time to pit and get back on track ahead of Schumacher. Although technically legal, the Ferrari move was widely condemned, especially by Williams

technical director Patrick Head, who raced down the pit lane and angrily berated the Ferrari officials. Their unconvincing explanation was that Salo had slowed to conserve fuel.

Irvine cruised safely over the line three seconds ahead of Schumacher to gain the extra point. Williams could take comfort in the fact that Alex Zanardi was at last coming to grips with his car, and would have been in the points if he had not had to pit an extra time because of refuelling problems during his first stop.

Jordan ran much the same race they had run in Hungary, with Hill again claiming sixth and Frentzen again coming in third. Frentzen's point scoring made a surprisingly consistent pattern; he had crossed the line in either third or fourth place in every race since his victory in France. Beside racking up points for Jordan, he has steadily climbed up the driver's

The Ferraris of Irvine and Salo go into the steep climb of Eau Rouge.

table. After their spectacular troubles during qualifying, BAR were able to celebrate: for the first time in 12 races, Jacques Villeneuve managed to finish a race. He was in 15th place, just ahead of Gené's tail-ending Minardi, but it was at least a start.

B E T W E E N   T H E   R A C E S

30 August Ecclestone axes Spa for 2000 season

Bernie Ecclestone has announced that Spa-Francorchamps has been removed from the list of grand prix venues for next season. In the weeks leading up to the 1999 race, Ecclestone and Belgian Economics Minister Serge Kubla failed to agree on a compromise over the Belgian government's complete ban on tobacco advertising. Consequently, the cars were forced to race without their usual tobacco advertising slogans, much to the displeasure of the Formula One establishment, which relies heavily on the revenues provided by the tobacco industry.

Spa is considered by many to be the best circuit in Formula One, and its loss will be felt by drivers and spectators alike. Unless there is a turnaround in the Belgian authorities' attitude towards the tobacco ban, it is possible that the Dutch Zandvoort circuit, which has recently been awarded an F1 testing licence, will replace Spa for 2000.

30 August Ferrari boss criticizes team for Belgian failure

Luca di Montezemolo, the Ferrari chairman, held his team responsible for Ferrari's poor performance at Spa this weekend, focussing his anger on the engineering department. After a meeting with the Ferrari engineers, Di Montezemolo said: "If the drivers don't have the car, they can't win. And at Spa, they didn't have the car. We have to believe in this championship, so I'm calling now for the fullest possible technical support for the drivers." Throughout the weekend, Eddie Irvine had complained that his car did not have the necessary speed or the right set-up to be competitive.

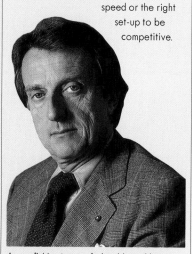

Luca di Montezemolo has blamed his engineering team for Ferrari falling behind McLaren in the Constructors' Championship.

31 August Hakkinen admits it was his mistake at first corner

Although clearly disappointed by the result of the Belgian Grand Prix, Mika Hakkinen has reluctantly accepted that team-mate David Coulthard was not to blame for their coming together at the first bend. "I can see now that David was ahead," said Hakkinen, "and had the right to turn in when he did. There is no problem between us over the incident."

No West insignia could be shown on McLaren's equipment at Spa, the result of a blanket ban on tobacco advertising.

On the previous day, McLaren team principal Ron Dennis had come down firmly on Coulthard's side regarding who was to blame for the incident. Following the race, Dennis and the drivers, along with Mercedes sports chief Norbert Haug, met to discuss the incident. After the meeting, Dennis reported their findings: "It was clearly Mika's fault. Mika made a mistake and he was very lucky all it cost him was the first corner, because he was very lucky he didn't end up with a stop-go penalty as well."

Dennis underlined once more the McLaren philosophy of allowing each driver to race to the best of his ability. He said: "People think they are loose words when we say we let our drivers battle for the championship, but they aren't, as we all saw."

2 September Schuey will not race at Monza

Any Ferrari hopes that Michael Schumacher would return to racing for the Italian Grand Prix were dashed after the German driver tested again at Monza. He completed 24 laps of the high-speed circuit but afterwards complained that he still felt excessive pain while driving on the track. Adoring fans clustered around the track with banners calling for his return, but Schumacher said: "I am not yet capable of driving at my maximum ability, therefore there is not even any point in continuing to test over the next couple of days." It is increasingly certain that Schumacher will not contemplate a return to racing until after the European Grand Prix on 26 September.

4 September $48 million required to join Formula One

A new proposal, which will be submitted to the FIA World Council in October, states that any new team wishing to enter Formula One will have to put up a $48 million (£30 million) bond. This will act as a deposit to prevent under-funded teams from going bankrupt in mid-season. The bond will be paid back to the team on the basis of $4 million a month during the course of the year. At present there is space for a further team to join the existing 11, and Toyota and General Motors have both expressed interest in participating in Formula One.

6 September Early retirement for Hill – again?

Rumours are circulating that Damon Hill could step down even before the current season ends. The Jordan team's stated aim for 1999 was to finish third in the constructor's championship table, and only a bizarre mishap will prevent this from coming about. Hill had always said that he would continue with Jordan to ensure this position, but with team-mate Heinz-Harald Frentzen's excellent record this season, no further contribution is required.

The fine art of the F1 start

GIVEN THE DIFFICULTY OF overtaking on most Formula One tracks, a good grid placing is vitally important. Accidents apart, the driver who has pole position, especially at circuits such as Monaco and Hungary, is likely to be first past the chequered flag. After the end of qualifying, the best time for a driver to influence a race is during the first few seconds.

Countdown to the off

Once the pit lane has closed and the drivers have made their formation lap, weaving from side to side to warm up tyres and braking hard to get brake temperatures up to their optimum levels, the cars line up on the grid. This is a very tense moment for any driver. His visor goes down, the engine revs up, and he sees the five starting lights going on at one-second

The moment when the five red lights suddenly go out is perhaps the most tense for Formula One drivers.

Above: Popular in America, rolling starts minimize accidents but are less spectacular than standing starts.

Left: The risk of collision is greatest in the seconds following the start.

intervals. Despite the thunderous roar of 22 high-performance engines, the driver's mind is totally focussed on the moment all the lights go off together, signalling that the start has begun.

The engine/transmission systems in F1 cars are unforgiving and make getting off the grid a far from easy proposition. As Michael Schumacher found out at Suzuka last season, unless engine revs are held at just the right level the car is likely to stall (and be sent to the back of the grid). The technique behind a fast start is very

simple in theory: to apply the engine's power directly to the wheels with maximum efficiency. In practice this is far more difficult. Over-acceleration or letting out the clutch too quickly causes wheelspin. This may look spectacular, but as the smoke billows out from behind the driver's rear wheels it signals poor power-to-track transmission, allowing others to pass before the car gets going.

More restrained starts tend to be more controlled and faster and, once the driver has successfully transmitted

the vast power of his F1 engine to the track, he can begin the dash to the first corner. For the driver in pole, the job is to get away smoothly and block attempts by others to get past him. For the rest, it is a double process of overtaking front runners and blocking those behind. In the melee of the first few seconds, fast starters fight to overcome those slow off the mark, while cars with light fuel loads hope to get past more heavily laden cars.

Although 22 cars charging out at maximum speed in a confined space

is cause enough for accidents, crunch time often comes at the first-corner bottleneck. The leaders normally negotiate this hazard fairly easily – although not always, as Hakkinen and Coulthard showed at Spa – but the main body of the pack concertinas dangerously: cars at the back continue to accelerate into the middle order, which is still in the process of braking hard for the bend. Multiple accidents are common as a result, but, of course, that is all part of the tension and excitement of an F1 start.

Italian Grand Prix

Italy has not been lucky for Mika Hakkinen this year. He spun off at Imola earlier in the season and then managed to repeat the process at Monza. While his disasters in Austria and Germany could be put down to external forces, the failures in Italy were Hakkinen's own fault — two lapses of concentration that may have cost him the championship. But one man's misfortune is another's gain, and Heinz-Harald Frentzen and Jordan were there to take victory, coming up from behind to join front runners McLaren and Ferrari as a possible contender for the title.

Unforced driver error caused Mika Hakkinen to spin out of the race on lap 30.

The Circuit

Monza

The Italian Grand Prix has been held at the Autodromo Nazionale di Monza every year since 1950, apart from one GP which was staged in 1980 at Imola. Monza is the fastest circuit in Formula One, in spite of its many chicanes. Engine power is very important. Drivers maximize their speed on the long straights by operating with very little wing, but the price is reduced ground adhesion on the slower sections of the circuit.

Track length 5.769 km (3.585 miles)
Race distance 305.775 km (190.005 miles) — 53 laps
1998 winner Michael Schumacher, Ferrari
Lap record 1:24.808 min, Mika Hakkinen, McLaren-Mercedes, 1997

Curva Grande
Variante 1
Variante 2
Variante Ascari
Curva del Serraglio
Curve di Lesmo
Curva Parabolica

Race Result

	Driver	Time
1	Frentzen	1:17.02.923
2	R. Schumacher	1:17.06.195
3	Salo	1:17.14.855
4	Barrichello	1:17.20.553
5	Coulthard	1:17.21.085
6	Irvine	1:17.30.325

Drivers' Championship

	Driver	Points
1	Hakkinen	60
=	Irvine	60
3	Frentzen	50
4	Coulthard	48
5	M. Schumacher	32
6	R. Schumacher	30
7	Barrichello	15
8	Fisichella	13

Salo, 10 pts. Hill, 7 pts. Wurz, Diniz, 3 pts. Herbert, Panis, 2 pts. De la Rosa, Alesi, Trulli, 1 pt.

Constructors' Championship

	Constructor	Points
1	McLaren-Mercedes	108
2	Ferrari	102
3	Jordan-Mugen-Honda	57
4	Williams-Supertec	30
5	Stewart-Ford	17
6	Benetton-Playlife	16

Sauber, 4 pts. Prost, 3 pts. Arrows, 1 pt.

More power to the Jordan challenge

Qualification

Mika Hakkinen put in a stunning third flying lap to take his 11th pole of the season so far — it was the fastest lap ever driven around the Monza circuit in its present configuration, and in a car supposedly lacking the speed of its predecessors. Hakkinen was visibly delighted: "The qualifying session was one of the most enjoyable — I couldn't believe I was able to bang in that time."

Williams elbow forward

McLaren's David Coulthard was less pleased, especially when his bid for a front-row place was dashed by a fine performance from Heinz-Harald Frentzen. But Williams had reason to be pleased with their drivers, who were placed fourth and fifth on the grid. Interestingly, Zanardi out-qualified his team-mate Ralf Schumacher, reflecting a new-found confidence in his car.

Indifferent Ferrari

Ferrari had a fairly wretched day, with Eddie Irvine able to secure only eighth on the grid, a full second and a half behind Hakkinen. Ferrari had clearly fallen behind McLaren in terms of speed, although Mika Salo was able to gain a place alongside Schumacher on the third row. At the back of the grid, the Italian Minardi team beat Arrows, who ran poorly through lack of testing.

Qualifying Times

1	Hakkinen	McLaren-Mercedes	1:22.432
2	Frentzen	Jordan-Mugen-Honda	1:22.926
3	Coulthard	McLaren-Mercedes	1:23.177
4	Zanardi	Williams-Supertec	1:23.432
5	R Schumacher	Williams-Supertec	1:23.636
6	Salo	Ferrari	1:23.657
7	Barrichello	Stewart-Ford	1:23.739
8	Irvine	Ferrari	1:23.785
9	Hill	Jordan-Mugen-Honda	1:23.979
10	Panis	Prost-Peugeot	1:24.016
11	Villeneuve	BAR-Supertec	1:24.188
12	Trulli	Prost-Peugeot	1:24.293
13	Alesi	Sauber-Petronas	1:24.591
14	Wurz	Benetton-Playlife	1:24.593
15	Herbert	Stewart-Ford	1:24.594
16	Diniz	Sauber-Petronas	1:24.596
17	Fisichella	Benetton-Playlife	1:24.862
18	Zonta	BAR-Supertec	1:25.114
19	Badoer	Minardi-Ford	1:25.348
20	Gené	Minardi-Ford	1:25.695
21	De la Rosa	Arrows	1:26.383
22	Takagi	Arrows	1:26.509

Throughout most of F1 1999, the battle for supremacy has raged between McLaren and Ferrari. The normal pattern of events has dictated that if the McLarens have problems, then the top places are taken by Ferrari. But the later races have seen a change in the pattern. Consistent point-scoring by Frentzen, helped by his win at Monza, has brought Jordan into contention. Williams, too, have made very impressive advances and now have the potential to get drivers onto the podium. How the championship will end is increasingly uncertain.

David Coulthard had one of his bad-start days, being passed by Williams' Alex Zanardi and Ralf Schumacher, before falling prey to Mika Salo's Ferrari. This was to be a disappointing race for McLaren's Scottish driver, especially when he was overtaken again as a result of a fine passing move by Rubens Barrichello on lap 11.

At the front, however, everything seemed to be going well for McLaren, as Hakkinen got away quickly, with

Hakkinen plainly suffered agonies of self-recrimination after his error.

Frentzen's Jordan behind. The Jordan driver was unable to keep up with Hakkinen, who began to build up a steady lead. By lap 28 Hakkinen was a fairly comfortable eight seconds ahead of Frentzen, but McLaren had put out the "push" signal on the pit board. Whether this affected the Finnish driver is hard to say, but disaster struck at the first chicane on the following lap. Hakkinen tried to flick his gear paddle down to second gear — the

appropriate one for the corner — but in the process overdid it, and engaged first instead. At such a speed his rear wheels locked immediately, and the car spun off the track with a stalled engine. Hakkinen had eliminated himself from the race and after the incident was clearly distraught.

More mayhem had occurred earlier in the race when the Arrows car of Tora Takagi ran into the back of Luca Badoer's Minardi. In the

Above: Ralf Schumacher zooms ahead of Williams team-mate Alex Zanardi, who had chivalrously waved him through after car damage put an end to his own hopes of a top placing. Right: Tora Takagi's Arrows car climbs aboard the Minardi driven by Luca Badoer.

accident, which the Japanese driver called a "touching of wheels", Takagi drove straight over the Minardi, forcing it out of the race. Minardi boss Gabriele Rumi was furious at the loss of Badoer and hinted darkly that this was a deliberate Arrows' tactic.

Williams team spirit

Alex Zanardi, who at last had come to terms with the twitchy aerodynamics of his Williams, seemed set for a good race. Behind Frentzen, he was well ahead of team-mate Schumacher, but on lap 16 he was forced to slow as a result of damage to the car floor. Schumacher began to press Zanardi. On the following lap, Schumacher was waved through by the Italian, for which he was duly grateful. When asked after the race whether his team had signalled Zanardi to move over, Schumacher replied: "No, we have an agreement that if one or the other of us is quicker, we don't hold each other, we help each other."

After the single series of pit-stops that were made by all the teams (with the exception of Prost), the race settled down. Frentzen held the lead with Schumacher second, followed by Salo, then Barrichello, Coulthard, and Irvine. These positions remained the

Frentzen adds the Monza trophy to the one he gained at Magny-Cours.

Heinz-Harald Frentzen's Jordan paints the Monza circuit yellow.

same to the chequered flag, although Salo tried to close on Schumacher and set a number of very fast laps in the process. But Schumacher effectively countered by achieving the fastest lap of all (at just over 150 mph) and saw off the Ferrari challenge.

But the day ended primarily as a triumph for Jordan: not only had the team won its second race of the season, but Eddie Jordan's 14-1 outside bet on Frentzen to win had brought its own financial reward. And with his win at Monza, Frentzen joined Hakkinen, Irvine, and Coulthard on the list of hopefuls for the championship.

BETWEEN THE RACES

Souvenir hunters stripped *Fisichella's Benetton during an outbreak of disorder at Monza.*

13 September *Fans run amok at Monza race track*

Italian race authorities have angrily censured the behaviour of drunken race fans at the Italian Grand Prix. Before the race, a mass brawl broke out between rival groups and 95 people were injured in the ensuing riot, although only two needed hospital treatment. Hundreds of bottles were thrown onto the race track, and fans without tickets clashed with security guards in an attempt to break into the circuit. At the end of the race, souvenir hunters climbed over the track barriers and began to ransack the Benetton of Giancarlo Fisichella, which was parked at the first corner. Although armed police were finally able to drive off the scavengers, the Benetton suffered extensive damage. The team may take legal action against the race organizers.

13 September *Minardi may have to quit Formula One*

After both Minardi cars failed to complete the Italian Grand Prix yesterday, team boss and founder Giancarlo Minardi said the future of the team depended on finding a major sponsor for next year. The team have been in consultation with the Spanish telecom giant Telefonica throughout most of the season. Telefonica are already a major sponsor of Minardi – exploiting their connection with Spanish driver Marc Gené – and may wish to buy the team outright. "We're in talks with Telefonica," confirmed Minardi, "as well as others with the view to either selling out or finding a main supporter. Anything is possible."

14 September *TV rights to go out to tender*

In response to the EU's investigation into the assignment of television rights within Formula One, the FIA is looking at ways of selling the rights on the open market. Formerly, F1 TV rights were handed over to the Formula One Administration, a company owned by Bernie Ecclestone – an arrangement the EU believed was anti-competitive. Although an open sale would appease the EU, it is unlikely that any other organization could rival the resources and expertise boasted by Ecclestone's company.

16 September *Newey move to Ferrari denied*

McLaren's famed technical director Adrian Newey has become the subject of rumours that he might be contemplating a move to Ferrari, replacing Rory Byrne as chief

McLaren technical mastermind *Adrian Newey denies plans to move to Ferrari.*

designer. Newey was seen having lunch with Luca di Montezemolo, chairman of Ferrari, and sporting director Jean Todt at a restaurant in Maranello. Newey, however, denied the rumour, saying that,

while he received offers from other teams, his contract with McLaren still stood and he was happy in his job. Todt's response to the story was rather more forthright: "It's bullshit!"

24 September *Schumacher's version of events*

Sidelined Ferrari star Michael Schumacher has been making his predictions as to the likely winner of the world championship. As ever, the German maestro's comments were full of meaning, intended as much to unnerve his rivals as elucidate the situation. Schumacher said he thought that Hakkinen should claim the title as long as he stopped making mistakes. "Mika has given a lot of presents to our team," Schumacher commented. "We will have to see how many more presents they will be handing out to the end of the season."

As for his own team, it is clear that Schumacher would feel somewhat less than ecstatic if they were to win the championship without his help. His view is straightforward: "Ferrari are missing technical development because the car is simply not as good as the McLaren. I can't say how much better the car would have been if I had still been there." Irvine was quick to respond to Schumacher's remarks: "What Michael says is not important. Obviously, he has less faith in Ferrari than I do. I know my mechanics, engineers, and the whole team has never stopped working for me. And they never stopped working for Michael."

24 September *A prince bows out*

Arrows have announced at Germany's Nürburgring that Prince Malik Ado Ibrahim is resigning from his managerial post with the team. Malik bought a 20 per cent stake in Arrows at the beginning of the season, and was instrumental in securing the financial backing of the Morgan Grenfell bank. But the reason for the African prince's departure is thought to lie in his failure to bring in promised sponsorship deals to the team. In addition, it is believed that Malik's T-Minus range of sports products, advertised on the Arrows cars, has failed to produce the revenue necessary to make his position at Arrows commercially viable.

Tough times for Ferrari

In the first half of the season, Ferrari were able to maintain their challenge against McLaren. While they lacked the speed of McLaren in qualifying, they were only a fraction behind, and were usually able to make up the difference during the race itself. In the last few races, however, the Italian team have faltered. The last decent qualifying time achieved by Ferrari was at Hungary, where Irvine started the race sandwiched between the cars of Hakkinen and Coulthard.

Part of Ferrari's problem lies in the growing strength of Jordan and Williams, with Frentzen and Ralf Schumacher now coming between the

Ferrari sporting director Jean Todt, now bereft of his star driver.

McLarens and Ferraris on the grid. But the question remains, if McLaren can hold off the newcomers, why is Ferrari failing so badly? And, technology aside, why has the superbly drilled Ferrari race team become ragged at times, most notably at the European GP?

The management at Ferrari angrily deny any loss of interest in the championship after Michael Schumacher's accident, although Ross Brawn admits they have suffered from not having the German driver's technical input over the last few races. In their defence,

Ross Brawn valued Schumacher's technical grasp.

Ferrari also make the point that the circuits at Spa and Monza do not suit their cars. On the other hand, they should have qualified better at a high downforce track like the Nürburgring. Whatever the reason, the Scuderia is not on the pace.

When stakes are high, so are the pressures

Damon Hill, slumped and dejected after spinning off at Silverstone in 1996, endured critical comparison with Michael Schumacher.

With the championship within reach, Mika Hakkinen must keep his grip.

During the final races of the 1999 F1 season – in a championship that has produced no outright leader – there is immense pressure on the top drivers to perform at nothing less than the peak of their ability. This is the time when mistakes are made, and when the mistakes matter most. To make things worse, drivers and team managers are waging a relentless psychological war to undermine their rivals. Mika Hakkinen admitted that it was probably this pressure that caused his mistake at the Italian

Grand Prix, which, in turn, may have had a knock-on effect on his performance at the Nürburgring.

In the recent past, Damon Hill, while a driver for Williams, suffered when critics set his achievements against the brilliance of Michael Schumacher at Benetton. These judgments certainly affected Hill's confidence and performance, although in the end he was able to come back to win a world championship.

Perhaps the greatest psychological strain for a driver comes from his team-mate. The two men race the same car and, if given the same team support, they are equal, except in the crucial matter of talent. And when one driver is clearly faster than the other, the slower man comes under intense scrutiny. Some obviously strong drivers – such as David Coulthard and Johnny Herbert – are able to handle this, but others begin to crumble and lose their conviction.

Mika Hakkinen leads by the narrowest of margins in the final run-in to the championship – but how well can he take the pressure?

26 SEPTEMBER • NÜRBURGRING

European Grand Prix

Holding high the European Grand Prix constructors' trophy, Jackie Stewart is flanked by Johnny Herbert (1st place) and Rubens Barrichello (3rd place).

The four contenders for the title — Hakkinen, Irvine, Frentzen, and Coulthard — seemed determined not to win at the Nürburgring. Out of this championship quartet, only Hakkinen managed to gain any points, and that only after a push towards the end. As in France, rain made this one of the most exciting races of the season. There were five different leaders during the race, and it was 200-1 outsider Johnny Herbert who led when the chequered flag came down. This may not have been a grand prix for the F1 connoisseur, but for sheer thrills and spills it was hard to beat. And once again, the race for the championship remained tantalizingly open.

Main picture: Pedro Diniz was lucky to escape with only minor injury after his Sauber was catapulted into the air by contact with Wurz's Benetton.

Track length 4.556 km
(2.831 miles)

Race distance 300.696 km
(186.848 miles) — 66 laps

1998 winner Mika Hakkinen,
McLaren-Mercedes

Lap record 1:18.805 min, Heinz-Harald
Frentzen, Williams-Renault, 1997

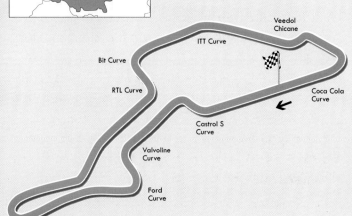

- Veedol Chicane
- ITT Curve
- Bit Curve
- RTL Curve
- Coca Cola Curve
- Castrol S Curve
- Valvoline Curve
- Ford Curve
- Dunlop Corner

The Circuit

Today's Nürburgring occupies an area of the Nordschliefe circuit in the Eifel mountains, which for 50 years was the world's most spectacular and dangerous course. The modern track is designed for Formula One racing; the tight Castrol S bend just after the finishing line is the scene of many mishaps, and the bends at RTL and Coca Cola also provide excitement.

Race Result

	Driver	Time
1	Herbert	1:41.54.314
2	Trulli	1:42.16.933
3	Barrichello	1:42.17.180
4	R. Schumacher	1:42.33.822
5	Hakkinen	1:42.57.264
6	Gené	1:42.59.468

Drivers' Championship

	Driver	Points
1	Hakkinen	62
2	Irvine	60
3	Frentzen	50
4	Coulthard	48
5	R. Schumacher	33
6	M. Schumacher	32
7	Barrichello	19
8	Fisichella	13
9	Herbert	12
10	Salo	10

Trulli, Hill, 7 pts. Wurz, Diniz, 3 pts.
Panis, 2 pts. De la Rosa, Alesi, Gené, 1 pt.

Constructors' Championship

	Constructor	Points
1	McLaren-Mercedes	110
2	Ferrari	102
3	Jordan-Mugen-Honda	57
4	Williams-Supertec	33
5	Stewart-Ford	31
6	Benetton-Playlife	16
7	Prost-Peugeot	9
8	Sauber-Petronas	4

Arrows, Minardi-Ford, 1 pt.

Herbert makes history for Stewart

Qualification

The circuit in the Eifel mountains was wet after a pre-session shower, and all the teams were in a quandary whether to put in a banker lap in case it rained again, or wait as long as possible for the track to dry out. The person who made the best judgment was Heinz-Harald Frentzen. He was confident that the Jordan had the speed to get to the front row as long as the conditions were right. While the Jordan team were trying to force Frentzen onto the track, Frentzen refused point-blank. He called the shots, and after a slow circuit-tester on a dry set-up he set a blistering lap in the final minutes of the session to put him on pole.

Ferrari falling back

The McLarens followed the Jordan on to the grid, with Coulthard positioned ahead of his team-mate for a change. Ralf Schumacher's run of good form continued with him securing fourth place. Ferrari saw no let-up in their struggle against adversity, however, with Irvine only managing ninth — not a position from which he could realistically hope to challenge his championship rivals, who had taken the first three places. Ferrari's choice of harder tyres was part of the problem, although it was possible that Irvine might have got near the front runners if he hadn't spun in his final flying lap.

Qualifying Times

1	Frentzen	Jordan-Mugen-Honda	1:19.910
2	Coulthard	McLaren-Mercedes	1:20.176
3	Hakkinen	McLaren-Mercedes	1:20.376
4	R. Schumacher	Williams-Supertec	1:20.444
5	Panis	Prost-Peugeot	1:20.638
6	Fisichella	Benetton-Playlife	1:20.781
7	Hill	Jordan-Mugen-Honda	1:20.818
8	Villeneuve	BAR-Supertec	1:20.825
9	Irvine	Ferrari	1:20.842
10	Trulli	Prost-Peugeot	1:20.965
11	Wurz	Benetton-Playlife	1:21.144
12	Salo	Ferrari	1:21.314
13	Diniz	Sauber-Petronas	1:21.345
14	Herbert	Stewart-Ford	1:21.379
15	Barrichello	Stewart-Ford	1:21.490
16	Alesi	Sauber-Petronas	1:21.634
17	Zonta	BAR-Supertec	1:22.267
18	Zanardi	Williams-Supertec	1:22.284
19	Badoer	Minardi-Ford	1:22.631
20	Gené	Minardi-Ford	1:22.760
21	Takagi	Arrows	1:23.401
22	De la Rosa	Arrows	1:23.698

Johnny Herbert gave his boss the prize of a lifetime as he brought the tartan-badged Stewart car home in first place. Renowned as the unluckiest man in F1, this was for him a dramatic, and richly deserved, change of fortune. His team shared the good luck; in just 50 grands prix they achieved first place, a very respectable tally when compared to Jordan's 127 races before their first win.

The first event of this incident-packed race occurred on the first corner. Hill's Jordan lost power; Wurz braked hard behind Hill but in the process nudged the Sauber of Diniz, which almost immediately became airborne, then flipped upside down and crashed hard on the ground. Worryingly, the roll hoop was crushed and for a moment it looked as though Diniz may have been badly hurt. Very fortunately, the car's high cockpit sides prevented any

A scooter had to serve after electrical failure ended Frentzen's European GP.

By spinning off, Coulthard effectively wrote himself off as world champion.

serious damage and he emerged with only minor neck and leg injuries.

Just as the race was settling down with Frentzen holding his lead, followed by Hakkinen, Coulthard, and Ralf Schumacher, the rain started. Hakkinen was the first in to change to wets, but for once McLaren misread the situation; the rain was affecting only part of the track and Hakkinen began to lose track position. The Finn seemed to lose interest in the race, even allowing himself to be overtaken by Marc Gené's Minardi.

Frentzen and Coulthard came in together on lap 32 for their scheduled pit-stops. The Jordan burst out just ahead of the McLaren, but at the next corner it ambled to a halt with electrical failure, Frentzen pounding the wheel in frustration.

Coulthard slides out

The lead now passed to Coulthard, who pulled away from Schumacher in what remained extremely difficult conditions: one moment the track was drying out, but a little while later it was wet again as more light rain began to fall. Coulthard pushed too hard and on lap 37 he found himself travelling across the gravel to gently nose into the tyre wall — 10 points and his chance of the championship gone.

Disaster had also struck Irvine. When he came in for new tyres on lap 21, he found the pit crew in disarray as a result of an unscheduled stop made by Mika Salo for a new nose. They had put away Irvine's tyres and when he came in they couldn't find

A burst tyre caused Ralf Schumacher to join the growing list of race leaders taken out by a major mishap.

the fourth wheel. For an agonizing 28 seconds, Irvine sat stationary until the missing wheel was found. Irvine, who had stood a good chance of a podium finish, was now in 13th place.

After Coulthard's spin, the lead passed to Ralf Schumacher, who was arguably handling the uncertain wet/dry conditions better than any other driver on the track. But just as the German thought he had secured the race, his right rear tyre punctured. With strips of rubber flying, his Williams limped back to the pits for new tyres. This lost Schumacher the

race, but he managed to rejoin the track sufficiently high up the order to cross the line in fourth, followed by a lately re-vitalized Mika Hakkinen.

The race concluded with a superb tussle at the front: Johnny Herbert led the Prost of Jarno Trulli, which was under pressure from Barrichello's Stewart. Trulli fought hard and fair to hold the otherwise faster Stewart, and his second place trebled Prost's point tally at a stroke. But the glory went to Herbert, who stayed calm throughout and correctly anticipated when to change from dry to wet tyres.

Prost on the podium, thanks to Trulli

Jarno Trulli is one of the most highly regarded of the new generation of F1 drivers, and at the Nürburgring he was able to demonstrate his abilities with a fine defensive drive against Rubens Barrichello. During his time at Prost, however, the car has let Trulli down on so many occasions that it has been hard to assess his real talent. But the move to Jordan next season will be his opportunity to show the world that he has what it takes to be a top driver.

A naturally gifted driver, Trulli demonstrated his skill at the Nürburgring.

Delighted at the wholly unexpected turn of events, the Stewart team cheer Johnny Herbert to their historic first Formula One win.

BETWEEN THE RACES

5 October BMW unveils new engine with track test

The new BMW V10 engine, which will provide the power-plant for the Williams team next season, has made its public debut at Austria's A1-Ring. Different versions of the engine were installed in two 1998 FW20 Williams cars. The first car suffered an oil leak from its engine and had to be brought back to the garage, so the other car, equipped with a more advanced version of the BMW V10, was used in its place.

Rumours have been circulating that the new BMW engine is overweight, unreliable, and lacking in power. If there is any truth in these reports, Williams, who have signed a five-year deal with BMW, will not have the engine they need to compete with the top teams. BMW, however, say they are not concerned by these rumours, and will develop an engine capable of taking on their main German rival, Mercedes.

7 October Spa back as new race calendar is published

A step-down by the government of Belgium, allowing the temporary continuation of tobacco advertising along the lines set by other European governments, has led to reinstatement of the Belgian Grand Prix at Spa-Francorchamps. Also, Magny-Cours, which, it was rumoured, had lost its place to the Paul Ricard circuit, will continue to host the French Grand Prix. The first grand prix of 2000 will be in Australia on 12 March, followed by the Brazilian Grand Prix on the 26th. The season will conclude with the Malaysian Grand Prix on 22 October.

7 October Renault to return to Formula One

Renault, whose engines dominated Formula One for much of the 1990s, have decided to return to the sport. The parent company have given Renault Sport the go-ahead to produce an engine that will compete with Mercedes, Ferrari, and Honda. It is possible that the engine could be badged as a Nissan, to improve the image of the loss-making Japanese motor manufacturer, in which Renault has a 35 per cent stake.

Not surprisingly, many teams have shown great interest in developing a tie-up with Renault. Benetton, who won a world championship with Renault in 1995, are desperate to find a top engine supplier, and would be prepared to be bought out at the right price. Prost will need

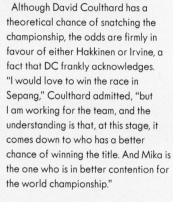

In BMW livery, an FW20 Williams is powered by the new BMW V10 engine at the A1-Ring.

Alain Prost may woo Renault in response to Peugeot's planned departure from F1.

a new engine partner to replace Peugeot, and a dynamic all-French line-up might prove attractive in the French market. As yet, Renault are refusing to comment on how they will re-enter F1, whether simply as an engine supplier or possibly as a team owner like Ford.

7 October Schumacher announces that he is fit to race again

Michael Schumacher has announced his intention to drive for Ferrari for the remaining two races of the season. For weeks Schumacher has been saying that a return to racing is out of the question, but after recent testing at Mugello he

has suddenly changed his mind. Whether this was solely his own decision or was influenced by pressure from the Ferrari team remains a matter for conjecture. Schumacher's decision was severely criticized by his manager, Willi Weber, who is adamant that Schuey's early return is too risky. "What happens if he has another accident?" Weber said. "He won't only be compromising his health, but also the next season."

14 October Coulthard promises to help Hakkinen in title race

Although David Coulthard has a theoretical chance of snatching the championship, the odds are firmly in favour of either Hakkinen or Irvine, a fact that DC frankly acknowledges. "I would love to win the race in Sepang," Coulthard admitted, "but I am working for the team, and the understanding is that, at this stage, it comes down to who has a better chance of winning the title. And Mika is the one who is in better contention for the world championship."

14 October Irvine demands help from Schumacher

Comments by Michael Schumacher that his main aim this season is to win the constructors' title for Ferrari, rather than help his team-mate win the world title, brought a swift response from Eddie Irvine: "As far as I am concerned, the main priority is to win the drivers' championship. Luca [di Montezemolo] has told me that the constructors' championship is not as important as the drivers' title. But let's hope we can win both because that would be a great way for me to finish what would be a fantastic four years with Ferrari."

Eddie Irvine would love to hand Ferrari the championship.

Are team orders good for Formula One?

WHETHER DRIVERS SHOULD BE obliged to race under team orders has always been one of the most hotly debated issues in Formula One. Typically, one driver of a team emerges as being faster than the other, and as the season progresses so the tactics of the team become focussed on the faster driver, the other man being enjoined by the team to act primarily in a supporting role.

In most teams this ascendancy is allowed to develop naturally, as at Jordan where Heinz-Harald Frentzen has proved far quicker than Damon Hill, despite the pre-season belief that Frentzen would have to complete a steep learning curve before being able to challenge his team-mate. At Ferrari, by contrast, team orders are established before the start of the season, with the number one driver contractually sure that his team-mate will support and defer to him from the first race onwards. McLaren have taken the opposite view, maintaining a team philosophy that both their drivers should be encouraged to race each other as vigorously as possible.

A question of tactics

The controversy over team orders centres on differing interpretations of what constitutes "fair racing". Those who support team orders claim that Formula One is a "team sport", saying that the two drivers should help each other to gain the best result for the team as a whole. Those who oppose team orders emphasize the "racing" aspect and think that drivers should race each other, regardless of team.

During this season, Ferrari tactics have aroused the ire of other teams. At the Belgian Grand Prix, for example, Patrick Head of Williams was furious at the manner in which Ferrari driver Mika Salo, who had been lapped by the field, appeared to hold up Ralf Schumacher deliberately and so prevent him from getting past Eddie Irvine. In contrast, McLaren have been widely praised for their sportsmanship, but competing team-mates can have a detrimental effect

By letting Irvine (right) into first place at Hockenheim, Mika Salo obeyed orders for the overall good of his team.

Intense rivalry is the order of the day for Hakkinen and Coulthard.

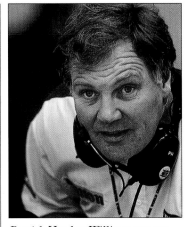

Patrick Head at Williams was not amused by Ferrari tactics at Spa.

on a team's overall success. Some observers believe that if Coulthard had been made to defer to Hakkinen, then Hakkinen would have been world champion several races ago.

In the past, Williams also suffered from letting both their drivers race each other to the finish. The Honda-powered Williams of 1986 was clearly the best car in F1 and won nine races,

which were split between Nigel Mansell (five) and Nelson Piquet (four). Although Williams easily walked away with the constructors' championship, the distribution of points between their two drivers allowed McLaren's Alain Prost to nip in and grab the drivers' championship by two points, despite the fact that he had won only four races.

For now, the FIA have decided that both approaches have a place in F1, so that while encouraging hard racing they do not punish teams for playing the team-orders card.

Malaysian Grand Prix

The inaugural Malaysian Grand Prix was expected to be a highlight of the season, and the spectacular return of Michael Schumacher to racing was almost enough to ensure that in itself. Driving a masterful defensive race, he denied Mika Hakkinen a higher place on the podium, while waving on Eddie Irvine to both the finishing line and a good chance of winning the championship in Japan. But Ferrari's pleasure in their one-two win was dashed when both cars were disqualified for illegal bodywork. Ferrari's appeal, set to be heard within a week, would ascertain whether there would be anything for them to play for at Suzuka.

While Eddie Irvine enjoyed a triumphal finish, both he and Michael Schumacher were soon battling against disqualification.

The Circuit

The brand-new Shah Alam circuit at Sepang has been constructed at great expense to provide a benchmark circuit for the future. It has a wide variation of bends requiring medium downforce settings. The wide track, and the long start-finish straight followed by turns 1 and 2, should provide good overtaking opportunities.

Sepang

Track length 5.542 km (3.444 miles)
Race distance 310.378 km (192.865 miles) — 56 laps
1998 winner None
Lap record None

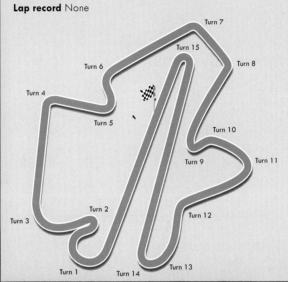

Race Result*

	Driver	Time
1	Irvine	1:36:38.494
2	M. Schumacher	1:36.39.534
3	Hakkinen	1:36.48.237
4	Herbert	1:36.56.032
5	Barrichello	1:37.10.790
6	Frentzen	1:37.13.378

Drivers' Championship*

	Driver	Points
1	Irvine	70
2	Hakkinen	66
3	Frentzen	51
4	Coulthard	48
5	M. Schumacher	38
6	R. Schumacher	33
7	Barrichello	21
8	Herbert	15
9	Fisichella	13
10	Salo	10

Trulli, Hill, 7 pts. Wurz, Diniz, 3 pts.
Panis, 2 pts. Alesi, De la Rosa, Gené, 1 pt.

Constructors' Championship*

	Constructor	Points
1	Ferrari	118
2	McLaren-Mercedes	114
3	Jordan-Mugen-Honda	58
4	Stewart-Ford	36
5	Williams-Supertec	33
6	Benetton-Playlife	16
7	Prost-Peugeot	9
8	Sauber-Petronas	4

Arrows, Minardi-Ford, 1pt.

* All results and points subsequent to Ferrari's successful appeal against disqualification.

Ferrari one-two runs into controversy

Qualification

From the moment he first climbed behind the wheel in Malaysia, Michael Schumacher showed his usual calm authority. On Saturday he clearly demonstrated his dominance over the rest of the field with one of the finest qualifying displays seen in recent years.

Fantastic Ferrari

A 1:40 lap was the benchmark that the top runners were aiming for, but only Schumacher was able to cross that barrier with a superb 1:39.688. The German's arrival rejuvenated the entire Ferrari team, and Eddie Irvine reversed his recent poor qualifying form by joining Schumacher on the front row, albeit nearly a second behind. The McLarens were struggling by comparison, although both drivers still made it onto the second row, Coulthard just ahead of Hakkinen.

Sterling Stewart

The recent good form of the Stewart team continued with excellent laps from Herbert, fifth, and Barrichello, sixth. More surprising was the poor showing by Jordan, with Hill in ninth and Frentzen far back in 14th place — the result of a spin in his opening qualifying lap. Williams too were off the pace, and Ralf Schumacher had to content himself with a place on the fourth row behind Wurz's Benetton.

Qualifying Times

1	M Schumacher	Ferrari	1:39.688
2	Irvine	Ferrari	1:40.635
3	Coulthard	McLaren-Mercedes	1:40.806
4	Hakkinen	McLaren-Mercedes	1:40.866
5	Herbert	Stewart-Ford	1:40.937
6	Barrichello	Stewart-Ford	1:41.351
7	Wurz	Benetton-Playlife	1:41.444
8	R Schumacher	Williams-Supertec	1:41.558
9	Hill	Jordan-Mugen-Honda	1:42.050
10	Villeneuve	BAR-Supertec	1:42.087
11	Fisichella	Benetton-Playlife	1:42.110
12	Panis	Prost-Peugeot	1:42.208
13	Zonta	BAR-Supertec	1:42.310
14	Frentzen	Jordan-Mugen-Honda	1:42.380
15	Alesi	Sauber-Petronas	1:42.522
16	Zanardi	Williams-Supertec	1:42.885
17	Diniz	Sauber-Petronas	1:42.933
18	Trulli	Prost-Peugeot	1:42.948
19	Gené	Minardi-Ford	1:43.563
20	De la Rosa	Arrows	1:43.579
21	Badoer	Minardi-Ford	1:44.321
22	Takagi	Arrows	1:44.637

Above: Unaware of the storm ahead, Schumacher and Irvine enjoy their win. Left: Hakkinen was in no mood for champagne-spraying.

McLaren were out-driven and out-thought by the Ferrari team. Michael Schumacher was kept on a one-stop pit strategy that enabled him to control the race by blocking Hakkinen, and in so doing protect Irvine from his main championship rival.

From the start, Schumacher led into the first corner and quickly built up a three-second lead before easing up on lap four to let Irvine overtake him. Schumacher soon found Coulthard in his rear mirrors. Gritting his teeth, the McLaren driver forced his way past the Ferrari. It was a potentially dangerous move that could have had both men off, but Coulthard demonstrated a fine line in controlled aggression and Schumacher was forced to accept that discretion can sometimes be the better part of valour. Ferrari's blocking strategy looked in peril for a while, especially when Coulthard set about reeling in Irvine. But fate was working against the Scot and fuel-pressure problems forced him to abandon on lap 15.

Red carpet for Irvine

Now Schumacher was acting as a buffer for Irvine against Hakkinen, allowing him to maintain position after the first round of pit-stops. The one-stopping Schumacher assumed the lead when Irvine pitted for a second time, but slowed again on lap 52 to let Irvine through for the final few laps to the chequered flag. Close behind the leaders, Herbert and Barrichello crossed the finishing line in fourth and fifth place respectively, earning more points for Stewart.

Schumacher had once more surprised his critics, many of whom doubted that he would play second fiddle to Irvine. But Schumacher played the good team-mate to the full and set up his former number two for a real chance of winning the championship for Ferrari. Irvine was full of praise for his fellow driver after the race: "This guy is depressing. Although he is the best number one, he is also the best number two. Michael was just amazing. He did all the hard work for me."

One centimetre: a critical measurement in Formula One

A barge board, fitted just below the Ferrari insignia.

Just two hours after Irvine and Schumacher had showered each other with victory champagne, technical delegate Joachim Bauer ruled that their cars did not conform to the FIA's technical regulations. Baseplates of the two aerodynamic deflector panels that channel air into the engine intakes — commonly known as barge boards — were found to be a centimetre short at the rear end. Bauer presented his findings to the FIA stewards, who accepted his ruling and disqualified both Ferraris from the race. Ferrari immediately lodged an appeal with the FIA.

Ferrari sporting director Jean Todt: the fault arose in machining.

Coulthard got past Schumacher by a bold challenge on the inside.

Hakkinen was hobbled by Schumacher's expertly obstructive driving.

Not everyone was so pleased. Ron Dennis, the Mercedes-McLaren team principal, bitterly attacked Ferrari's tactics, which he called "unsporting" and which had left Hakkinen stuck behind Schumacher for much of the race. Dennis was also angered by their decision to use scrubbed tyres that wore down to resemble grooveless slicks by the end of the race.

Hakkinen was generous in defeat. He commented: "It was the hardest race of my life. I was flat out all the way. Ferrari had brilliant tactics and I don't blame them. I spent most of the race behind Michael Schumacher and whilst I thought I could challenge him for the place I was unable to get past him. Part of the reason for this was that I had to drive very cautiously as I didn't want to get caught out by his inconsistent driving patterns. He was lifting in high-speed corners and fluctuating his speed so I had to be careful that I did not run into him."

It seemed a great comeback for Ferrari, but not for long. Disqualified within hours for illegal bodywork on both cars, the Scuderia would have to wait several nail-biting days before knowing the outcome of their appeal.

19 October *Ecclestone backs Ferrari appeal*

F1 boss Bernie Ecclestone has stated that he believes Ferrari's disqualification from the Malaysian GP to be misguided. He would prefer the battle for the title to carry over to the final race in Japan. Given Ecclestone's investment in televising the sport, his statement is not altogether surprising. "I have campaigned for years that Formula One rules and regulations are too tight," said Ecclestone. "It is bad for the sport. The public want to see a great finish to a great championship. It is a shame if the world championship could be decided by someone quite junior who has made a mistake in the factory." The appeal is to be held in Paris on Friday, 22 October.

FIA president Max Mosley announced to the world that Ferrari could keep their points after all.

20 October *Musical chairs as Panis tests for McLaren*

Former Prost driver Olivier Panis tested a McLaren-Mercedes at Magny-Cours today, posting the fastest time in a rain-soaked testing session. Since leaving F1, Panis has secured a ride with Mercedes in the German Touring Car series. In addition he has been taken on as a test driver for McLaren, eventually to take the place of Nick Heidfeld who is moving over to Prost next season.

As test driver for McLaren, Olivier Panis will be upgrading to Mercedes engines.

20 October *BAR promise staff bonus for improved performance*

British American Racing is desperate not to be last in the 1999 championship; they are the only team not to have scored a single point so far this year. In a bid to obtain at least one point, and get on a par with Minardi and Arrows, BAR boss Craig Pollock has offered each team member a personal bonus of £1000 if BAR finishes in the top ten.

Pollock's incentive is more than a matter of team honour, as BAR will receive $10 million in prize money and travelling expenses if they can lift themselves off the bottom of the championship table.

20 October *Stewart calls for Ferrari ban*

The Stewart team have stated that they will oppose any attempt to overturn Ferrari's disqualification at the appeal hearing in Paris. Stewart have taken up the offer to attend the hearing as the ban has moved Herbert and Barrichello to second and third place respectively. The extra five points from Malaysia has given Stewart an eight-point lead over Williams in the battle for fourth place in

the constructors' championship. A spokesman for the Stewart team said: "We feel that if Ferrari are found to have contravened the rules, then the disqualification should hold."

The FIA has reacted swiftly to distance itself from comments made by leading members of the sport, including Bernie Ecclestone, and has said that the five judges nominated to hear the appeal will be completely impartial. A statement read: "The FIA would like to stress that these judges will not be influenced by any outside opinion, irrespective of

the person who expresses it. They will decide the case solely on the basis of the evidence and arguments put forward during the hearing."

21 October *Minardi future secured by Spanish giant.*

The Spanish telecommunications giant Telefonica are believed to have agreed a $14 million sponsorship deal with Minardi, which also includes the services of Spanish driver Marc Gené. There had been rumours that

Telefonica pesetas will continue to flow into the Minardi coffers, and Gené keeps his place behind the wheel.

Telefonica might buy out the Italian team and move the whole operation to Spain, but this now seems highly unlikely. A tie-in with Toyota has also been floated, but if that happened at all it would not affect plans for the 2000 season. The Telefonica deal should secure the future of the team for next year, although Minardi have still to find an engine supplier and a second driver. Minardi had hoped to buy a Supertec engine, but Supertec boss Flavio Briatore has ruled that out.

23 October *Ferrari are reinstated for final battle in Japan*
The result was announced today of yesterday's appeal by Ferrari to have their disqualification from the Malaysian GP overturned. The ban on both team and drivers was lifted in a controversial decision that has delighted Ferrari but caused much displeasure to McLaren. The appeal was allowed because of anomalies in the measuring of car dimensions, and because Ferrari were able to provide an accurate jig of the barge board showing that it was within the permitted 5mm level of tolerance. Hakkinen will now travel to Japan four points behind Irvine, and will need to beat his Ferrari rival comprehensively to keep the title.

Mika Hakkinen reacted swiftly to the decision. "The crown may have been taken away from me," he said, "but I fully intend to win it back. There is everything to play for...The whole incident has just fired me up, and made me and the team even more determined to win."

Motor giants muscle in on F1

THE RELATIONSHIP BETWEEN the big motor manufacturers, who traditionally supply the engines for Formula One, and the racing teams has always been as crucial as it has been complex. A first-class engine can give a good team a decisive edge over their rivals, as was demonstrated by the total domination of Honda engines in the 1980s, regardless of whether they were used to power McLaren or Williams cars.

Power and the glory
In the past, motor manufacturers would ally themselves with teams as engine suppliers only. Ferrari, by comparison, remained an anomaly: a sports car manufacturer (owned by Fiat) who ran their own Formula One team using their own engine. In the last year, however, many of the motor conglomerates are showing an interest in taking over the running and ownership of F1 teams themselves.

The most striking example of this development has been Ford's well-trumpeted takeover of Stewart and its rebadging as Jaguar for next season. The growing public enthusiasm for Formula One has encouraged the car companies to become more involved in the sport as a means of promoting their brand name to a global market.

Battle of the marques
Ford boss Jac Nasser has made it plain that he wants Jaguar to have the same recognizable image as Ferrari. Jaguar are also determined to take on the might of Mercedes and BMW in their German homeland, and believe success in Formula One racing to be one of the best methods to achieve this aim. For their part, the German manufacturers have been conspicuous in promoting their own links with Formula One. Mercedes' relationship with McLaren has been transformed by their acquisition of a 40 per cent stake in the company in July 1999. And while BMW deny interest in owning Williams, rumours continue of a closer financial relationship growing between the two outfits.

Other players are moving into the sport. While Japanese car giant Honda have long been involved, their rival Toyota have announced plans to enter Formula One in 2002, designing and building their own car, which will be powered by a Toyota engine. They may wish to enter as a brand new team (there is an existing space for a twelfth team) or they may buy into an existing team. Renault also look likely to re-enter F1 within the next couple of years. It is rumoured that they may buy a small team, such as Arrows, and rebadge it as Nissan, in whom Renault have a major stake, thus introducing a third Japanese manufacture to F1.

No place for amateurs
Formula One has embraced the motor manufacturers because their material and financial support is essential if the teams are to hold their own in a world of rapidly escalating costs. This may of course lead to a loss of team identity, but whatever happens the structure of F1 motor sport is likely to change for ever.

Ron Dennis (right) and Norbert Haug: twin powers of McLaren-Mercedes.

Jackie Stewart confers with Martin Whittaker, boss of Ford Motorsport.

Japanese Grand Prix

Mika Hakkinen drove a faultless race to win the Japanese Grand Prix and the 1999 world drivers' championship. Starting four points behind title contender Eddie Irvine, Hakkinen was ably supported by his team and David Coulthard, who helped ensure that Irvine had no hope of getting to the front to make a challenge. Ferrari could take some consolation in winning the constructors' championship, their first since 1983, but the real jubilation lay with Hakkinen and McLaren. Irvine was gracious in defeat, saying: "Mika did a fantastic job today. He deserved the title and he won it in style."

Mika Hakkinen raises his fist in a heartfelt victory salute.

The Circuit

The Japanese Grand Prix was transferred from the old Fuji speedway track to Suzuka in 1987. The circuit is the only one in F1 to follow a figure-of-eight course and is popular with drivers, including Hakkinen and Schumacher. It offers a variety of hilly left and right turns and an equal balance of clockwise and anti-clockwise driving.

Suzuka

Triangle

Hairpin

'S' Curve

Degner Curve

Spoon Curve

Track length 5.864 km
(3.644 miles)
Race distance 310.807 km
(193.132 miles) — 53 laps
1998 winner Mika Hakkinen,
McLaren-Mercedes
Lap record 1:38.942 min,
Heinz-Harald Frentzen,
Williams-Renault, 1997

Race Result

	Driver	Time
1	Hakkinen	1:31.18.785
2	M. Schumacher	1:31.23.800
3	Irvine	1:32.54.473
4	Frentzen	1:32.57.420
5	R. Schumacher	1:32.58.279
6	Alesi	1 lap behind

Drivers' Championship

	Driver	Points
1	Hakkinen	76
2	Irvine	74
3	Frentzen	54
4	Coulthard	48
5	M. Schumacher	44
6	R. Schumacher	35
7	Barrichello	21
8	Herbert	15
9	Fisichella	13
10	Salo	10

Hill, Trulli, 7 pts. Diniz, Wurz, 3 pts.
Alesi, Panis, 2 pts. De la Rosa, Gené, 1 pt.

Constructors' Championship

	Constructor	Points
1	Ferrari	128
2	McLaren-Mercedes	124
3	Jordan-Mugen-Honda	61
4	Stewart-Ford	36
5	Williams-Supertec	35
6	Benetton-Playlife	16
7	Prost-Peugeot	9
8	Sauber-Petronas	5

Arrows, Minardi-Ford, 1pt.

Unstoppable Hakkinen races to victory

Qualification

The battle for perhaps the season's most important pole turned into a classic scrap between Ferrari and McLaren, Schumacher and Hakkinen repeatedly alternating best times. Schumacher finally put down a brilliant 1:37.470. As the session came to an end, Hakkinen went out on a last blinder and looked likely to beat Schuey, only to be stalled by Jean Alesi as he spun off in front of Hakkinen at the final chicane.

Irvine spins off

Behind the two leaders, David Coulthard had the edge over Eddie Irvine and qualified in third, a good position from which to block Hakkinen's main rival during the race. Irvine tried hard but suffered a heavy crash just before the hairpin. To increase Ferrari discomfiture, Heinz-Harald Frentzen squeezed into fourth, leaving Irvine on the third row. Irvine's position was far from hopeless, however, for if Schumacher won the race with Hakkinen in second, Irvine only needed fourth place or better to win the title.

Prost performance

Of the rest, the surprise came from the Prost team, one of the great under-performers of the year. Panis — without an F1 drive next year — stormed into sixth, followed by team-mate Trulli.

Qualifying Times

1	M Schumacher .Ferrari	1:37.470
2	Hakkinen ..... McLaren-Mercedes	1:37.820
3	Coulthard ... McLaren-Mercedes	1:38.239
4	Frentzen ...... Jordan-Mugen-Honda	1:38.696
5	Irvine .... Ferrari	1:38.975
6	Panis .... Prost-Peugeot	1:39.623
7	Trulli .... Prost-Peugeot	1:39.644
8	Herbert ...... Stewart-Ford	1:39.706
9	R Schumacher .. Williams-Supertec	1:39.717
10	Alesi .... Sauber-Petronas	1:39.721
11	Villeneuve .... BAR-Supertec	1:39.732
12	Hill .... Jordan-Mugen-Honda	1:40.140
13	Barrichello .... Stewart-Ford	1:40.140
14	Fisichella ..... Benetton-Playlife	1:40.261
15	Wurz .... Benetton-Playlife	1:40.303
16	Zanardi ..... Williams-Supertec	1:40.403
17	Diniz .... Sauber-Petronas	1:40.740
18	Zonta .... BAR-Supertec	1:40.861
19	Takagi ...... Arrows	1:41.067
20	Gené .... Minardi-Ford	1:41.529
21	De la Rosa ... Arrows	1:41.708
22	Badoer ...... Minardi-Ford	1:42.515

Once again the start was decisive, with Michael Schumacher pulling away slowly, sufficient to allow Hakkinen into the lead at the first corner. Although Hakkinen drove a superb race, Schumacher's performance was oddly muted for much of the time. He complained of handling problems at the start, but it was hard to escape the feeling that Schumacher was content to help Ferrari take the constructors' title and let Hakkinen win in Japan — leaving the ultimate prize of a Ferrari driver's victory for next season.

A crash during qualifying resulted in a disadvantageous grid placing for Irvine.

McLaren strategy called for Hakkinen to battle it out with Schumacher at the front, while Coulthard held up Irvine further down the field. But Olivier Panis — running on a light fuel load — surged through the traffic into third place, and Coulthard was sufficiently balked in the ensuing mêlée to allow Irvine into fourth. Panis did not last long, his gearbox giving up after 19 laps, but Irvine was a long distance behind the leaders when he moved up into third.

McLaren grab control

Coulthard was unable to pressurize Irvine on the track, so McLaren cannily brought their driver in early on lap 22 for a swift refuelling stop. Ferrari followed suit the next lap, but although both cars were stationary for 7.1 seconds, Coulthard succeeded in squeezing past Irvine as he exited the pit lane. McLaren now had control of the race, with Coulthard slowing down Irvine and blocking Frentzen and Ralf Schumacher close behind.

Later in the race, gear-change problems caused Coulthard to spin and damage the nose of his McLaren, although he was able to return to the pits for repairs. Back on track, DC was still struggling and briefly held up

Michael Schumacher, who was preparing to lap the McLaren driver. Schumacher was furious at the delay, and in a post-race outburst accused Coulthard of dangerous racing, also suggesting that Coulthard had deliberately collided with him at Spa last season. An angry Coulthard then threatened to sue Schumacher for his comments, although he admitted a dislike of defensive driving tactics.

The incident had no effect on the race outcome and McLaren, fearing

British hero Damon Hill proudly summarizes his racing achievements.

further problems, called Coulthard into retirement on lap 39 — effectively confirming Ferrari as constructors' champion. At the front, Hakkinen drove on without threat from Schumacher, in second place, or Irvine, a further 30 seconds behind. Irvine could only hope that Hakkinen would suffer mechanical failure or a catastrophic driver error. Neither happened, and Hakkinen cruised safely to victory, having lapped all but four of the remaining field.

Frentzen and Ralf Schumacher followed the leading trio over the line in fourth and fifth places respectively, and Alesi ended his stint with Sauber by earning a point for sixth place. The Stewarts just failed to win points, but they achieved their target of beating Williams to an overall fourth place.

Damon Hill's illustrious career in F1 ended with a whimper when, after spinning off, he simply drove back to the pits and retirement. But more disappointing was the failure of BAR to score a single point: finishing in last place in the championship, they face an uncertain future in the sport.

Mika Hakkinen was delighted at his win, and the fans appreciated Eddie Irvine's generosity in defeat.

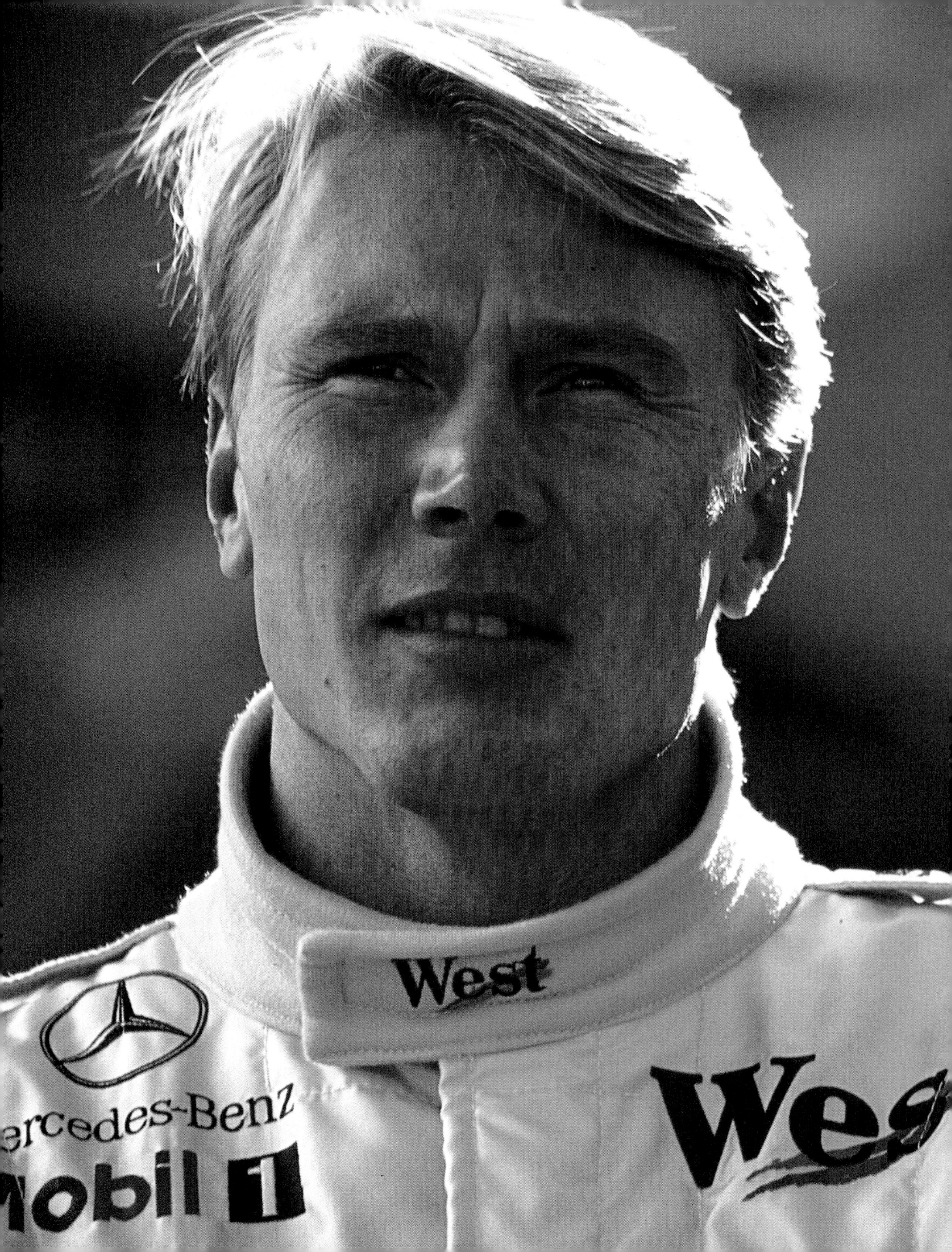
West
ercedes-Benz
obil 1

FIA world drivers' champion 1999

Hakkinen's road to the championship

Australian Grand Prix The season gets off to a disappointing start as Mika Hakkinen fails to finish. The only seeming consolation is that Michael Schumacher does not score any points, leaving his understudy Irvine to take the chequered flag.

Brazilian Grand Prix Hakkinen's victory at Interlagos compensates for the let-down in Australia, as he and Schumacher resume their duel of last year with Hakkinen in the ascendant.

French Grand Prix Although Heinz-Harald Frentzen takes the flag, Hakkinen is in second place, and thanks to victories in Spain and Canada he is able to build a small yet significant lead of eight points over Schumacher.

British Grand Prix Schumacher's accident transforms the season, and at the moment of the crash Hakkinen seems to have been gifted both the race and the title. But pit-lane disasters deprive Hakkinen of victory at Silverstone, and Irvine's second place brings a new contender to the fore.

Belgian Grand Prix The first-corner clash with David Coulthard forces Hakkinen into second place in a McLaren double victory. Although Hakkinen only loses four points, his angry reaction to the incident betrays telling signs of strain.

Italian Grand Prix The tricky circuit at Monza proves too much for Hakkinen. While comfortably in the lead, concentration fails him: he spins off and loses a crucial 10 points. Although the winner is Frentzen rather than Irvine, Hakkinen's distress is unmistakeable as he walks back to his team.

Malaysian Grand Prix In the mother of all controversies, Hakkinen is provisionally awarded the world championship following Ferrari's disqualification. But the appeal in Paris overturns the ruling, leaving Hakkinen four points behind Irvine. It is a hard blow for both team and driver.

Japanese Grand Prix Against all the odds, Hakkinen manages to defeat Irvine and Ferrari and win the title. It is an extraordinary race which confirms the Finn as a worthy world champion.

MIKA HAKKINEN BEGAN RACING in karts and won a number of championships in Finland before moving to Formula Ford in 1987. In his first year he won the European title, impressing observers as a naturally fast driver. After a move to Britain, he raced in Formula Three and won the championship in 1990 after a fierce duel with compatriot Mika Salo. He was given a seat with Lotus in Formula One in 1991, but apart from one third place his career did not thrive in that declining team.

A move to McLaren promised much, but then Ayrton Senna decided not to leave McLaren as expected. Hakkinen found himself the third driver behind Senna and Michael Andretti. It was a deeply frustrating time for the Finn, and even after Andretti's departure he remained in Senna's shadow. McLaren were themselves in the doldrums in the mid 1990s, but Hakkinen persevered with the team, despite a near-fatal accident in Australia in 1995.

After a slow start, the McLaren link-up with Mercedes began to transform the team's fortunes, and Hakkinen won his first grand prix at Jerez in 1997. The following season a confident Mika Hakkinen, driving a superb McLaren-Mercedes, fought a titanic battle with Schumacher to take the world championship. In 1999, any one of four drivers could have taken the championship, but in the end it became a direct contest between Hakkinen and Irvine, with the Finn just managing to scramble to victory at the last race in Japan.

DRIVERS' WORLD CHAMPIONSHIP

		Australia	Brazil	San Marino	Monaco	Spain	Canada	France	Britain	Austria	Germany	Hungary	Belgium	Italy	Europe	Malaysia	Japan	Total
1	Hakkinen	–	10	–	4	10	10	6	–	4	–	10	6	–	2	4	10	76
2	Irvine	10	2	–	6	3	4	1	6	10	10	4	3	1	0	10	4	74
3	Frentzen	6	4	–	3	–	0	10	3	3	4	3	4	10	–	1	3	54
4	Coulthard	–	–	6	–	6	0	–	10	6	2	6	10	2	–	–	–	48
5	M.Schumacher	0	6	10	10	4	–	2	–	–	–	–	–	–	–	6	6	44
6	R.Schumacher	4	3	–	–	2	3	3	4	–	3	0	2	6	3	–	2	35
7	Barrichello	2	–	4	0	–	–	4	0	–	–	2	0	3	4	2	0	21
8	Herbert	–	–	0	–	–	2	–	0	0	0	0	–	–	10	3	0	15
9	Fisichella	3	–	2	2	0	6	–	0	0	–	–	0	–	–	0	–	13
10	Salo	–	–	0	–	0	–	–	0	6	0	0	4	–	–	–	–	10
11	Hill	–	–	3	–	0	–	–	2	0	–	1	1	0	–	–	–	7
	=Trulli	–	–	–	0	1	–	0	0	0	–	0	0	–	6	–	–	7
13	Diniz	–	–	–	–	1	–	1	1	–	–	–	–	–	–	–	0	3
	=Wurz	–	0	–	1	0	–	0	2	0	0	0	–	–	0	0		3
15	Alesi	–	–	1	–	–	–	0	–	0	0	0	0	–	0	1		2
	=Panis	–	1	–	–	–	0	0	0	0	1	0	0	0	–	–		2
17	De la Rosa	1	–	–	–	0	–	0	–	–	–	0	–	–	–	0	1	1
	=Gené	–	0	0	–	–	0	0	0	0	0	0	–	1	0	–		1
NP	Badoer	–	0	–	–	0	0	–	0	0	0	–	–	–	–	–		0
	Sarrazin	–	–	–	–	–	–	–	–	–	–	–	–	–	–	–		0
	Takagi	0	0	–	–	0	–	–	0	–	–	–	–	–	–	–		0
	Villeneuve	–	–	–	–	–	–	–	–	0	0	0	–	0	0	–		0
	Zanardi	–	0	0	–	0	–	–	0	–	–	0	0	–	0	–		0
	Zonta	–	–	–	–	–	0	–	0	–	0	–	–	0	–	0		0

NP = no placing   0 = classified but no world championship points gained   – = retired or did not start
Points for drivers: first place: 10 points; second place: 6 points; third place: 4 points; fourth place: 3 points; fifth place: 2 points; sixth place: 1 point.

World champion drivers of F1

Year*	Driver/Team
1950	Giuseppe Farina/Alfa Romeo
1951	Juan Manuel Fangio/Alfa Romeo
1952	Alberto Ascari/Ferrari
1953	Alberto Ascari/Ferrari
1954	Juan Manuel Fangio/ Maserati-Mercedes
1955	Juan Manuel Fangio/Mercedes
1956	Juan Manuel Fangio/Ferrari
1957	Juan Manuel Fangio/Maserati
1958	Mike Hawthorne/Ferrari
1959	Jack Brabham/Cooper-Climax
1960	Jack Brabham/Cooper-Climax
1961	Phil Hill/Ferrari
1962	Graham Hill/BRM
1963	Jim Clark/Lotus-Climax
1964	John Surtees/Ferrari
1965	Jim Clark/Lotus-Climax
1966	Jack Brabham/Brabham-Repco
1967	Dennis Hulme /Brabham-Repco
1968	Graham Hill/Lotus-Ford
1969	Jackie Stewart/Matra-Ford
1970	Jochen Rindt/Lotus-Ford
1971	Jackie Stewart/Tyrell-Ford
1972	Emerson Fittipaldi/Lotus-Ford
1973	Jackie Stewart/Tyrell-Ford
1974	Emerson Fittipaldi/McLaren-Ford
1975	Niki Lauda/Ferrari
1976	James Hunt/McLaren-Ford
1977	Niki Lauda/Ferrari
1978	Mario Andretti/Lotus-Ford
1979	Jody Scheckter/Ferrari
1980	Alan Jones/Williams-Ford
1981	Nelson Piquet/Brabham-Ford
1982	Keke Rosberg/Williams-Ford
1983	Nelson Piquet/Brabham-BMW
1984	Niki Lauda/McLaren-Porsche
1985	Alain Prost/McLaren-Porsche
1986	Alain Prost/McLaren-Porsche
1987	Nelson Piquet/Williams-Honda
1988	Ayrton Senna/McLaren-Honda
1989	Alain Prost/McLaren-Honda
1990	Ayrton Senna/McLaren-Honda
1991	Ayrton Senna /McLaren-Honda
1992	Nigel Mansell/Williams-Renault
1993	Alain Prost/Williams-Renault
1994	Michael Schumacher/ Benetton-Ford
1995	Michael Schumacher/ Benetton-Renault
1996	Damon Hill/Williams-Renault
1997	Jacques Villeneuve/ Williams-Renault
1998	Mika Hakkinen/ McLaren-Mercedes
1999	Mika Hakkinen/ McLaren-Mercedes

* The world championship was held for the first time in 1950.

FIA world constructors' champion 1999

Ferrari's road to the championship

Australian Grand Prix Irvine's win puts Ferrari into an early lead in the constructors' title race. Although Schumacher suffers from technical problems, Ferrari demonstrate they have a reliability edge over McLaren.

Monaco Grand Prix Ferrari's first one-two of the season helps to open up a convincing 24-point lead over McLaren, who have been out-thought and out-driven by the Italian team.

French Grand Prix Poor Ferrari results in this and previous races in Canada and Spain allow McLaren to reduce Ferrari's lead to only six points.

British Grand Prix Schumacher's injury, caused by the crash into the tyre wall, rules him out of any serious attempt on the championship. Ferrari decide to persevere with their title ambition by backing Irvine and bringing in Mika Salo as Schumacher's replacement.

German Grand Prix Ferrari dominate the race with another fine one-two, which, when combined with the result in Austria, consolidates the team's overall lead to 19 points.

Belgian Grand Prix This race confirms that Ferrari have gone off the boil at this stage of the season. Ferrari president Luca di Montezemolo criticizes the team's engineers for failing to provide the drivers with sufficient power. For the first time this season, the lead passes to McLaren.

European Grand Prix Ferrari's slide continues, but their main rivals also put in poor performances.

Malaysian Grand Prix Schumacher's sudden return to racing rejuvenates the whole team. The two Ferraris qualify on the front row and easily win the race, only to be disqualified a few hours later. The successful appeal in Paris restores their lead over McLaren.

Japanese Grand Prix Ferrari prove the master of McLaren, winning their first constructors' title since 1983. Ironically, the team that bankrolled Schumacher for four seasons win the championship largely through the efforts of number two driver Eddie Irvine, who is leaving Ferrari for the new Jaguar team.

FERRARI ARE THE ONLY TEAM that have maintained a continuous presence in F1 since 1950. Perhaps as a result of their long history, Ferrari are guaranteed mass support, but such are the expectations of their fans that near impossible demands are made on the team to succeed.

Ferrari established a reputation for speed during close-fought battles in the 1950s with fellow Italian teams Alfa Romeo and Maserati, winning the drivers' championship with Ascari (1952 and 1953), Fangio (1956), and Hawthorn (1958). The Scuderia won both drivers' and constructors' titles in 1961 and 1964, before being overtaken by a new generation of teams such as Brabham, Lotus, and Tyrell.

Still controlled by founder Enzo Ferrari, the team had to wait until the mid 1970s for a renaissance. Austrian ace Niki Lauda led Ferrari to three successive constructors' titles from 1975 onwards. Competition became fiercer, but the team won the title again in 1979 and, guided by designer Harvey Posthlethwaite, they scored further success with constructors' world championships in 1982 and 1983. But this marked the high-water mark of Ferrari fortunes, because Formula One came to be dominated by McLaren and Williams for most of the next two decades.

In 1985 Michele Albereto, supported by Stefan Johansson, gave McLaren a good run for their money, and in 1990 Ferrari and Alain Prost got close to taking the title from Ayrton Senna and McLaren, but their hopes were thwarted by a collision in the last race of the season. These two attempts apart, Ferrari languished as one the better of the middle-order teams – clearly not what the *tifosi* demanded.

In the mid 1990s, under the leadership of Luca di Montezemolo, Ferrari once again tried to improve their fortunes. No expense was spared as the team tried to lose the chaotic image that had bedevilled their previous efforts to get on terms with McLaren and Williams. The break came at the beginning of 1996, when Ferrari lured Michael Schumacher to join the team. Twice world champion, Schumacher was the best driver in the field, and he brought with him from Benetton designer Rory Byrne and technical director Ross Brawn, both among the finest brains in F1.

The rival Renault-Williams cars proved a little too good for Ferrari, but an improving team managed second places in 1996 and 1997. Victory would almost certainly have come Ferrari's way in 1998 if they had not faced a McLaren team that was back in top form, with a car built by Adrian Newey and powered by an exceptional Mercedes engine.

In 1999, Ferrari parent company Fiat insisted that this must be the year of victory, Ferrari president Luca di Montezemolo stating that the team was "certain to win". In the last race of 1999, the president's promise of a ninth constructors' championship for Ferrari finally came through.

World champion constructors of F1

Year*	Team
1958	Vanwall
1959	Cooper-Climax
1960	Cooper-Climax
1961	Ferrari
1962	BRM
1963	Lotus-Climax
1964	Ferrari
1965	Lotus-Climax
1966	Brabham-Repco
1967	Brabham-Repco
1968	Lotus-Ford
1969	Matra-Ford
1970	Lotus-Ford
1971	Tyrell-Ford
1972	Lotus-Ford
1973	Lotus-Ford
1974	McLaren-Ford
1975	Ferrari
1976	Ferrari
1977	Ferrari
1978	Lotus-Ford
1979	Ferrari
1980	Williams-Ford
1981	Williams-Ford
1982	Ferrari
1983	Ferrari
1984	McLaren-TAG-Porsche
1985	McLaren-TAG-Porsche
1986	Williams-Porsche
1987	Williams-Honda
1988	McLaren-Honda
1989	McLaren-Honda
1990	McLaren-Honda
1991	McLaren-Honda
1992	Williams-Renault
1993	Williams-Renault
1994	Williams-Renault
1995	Benetton-Renault
1996	Williams-Renault
1997	Williams-Renault
1998	McLaren-Mercedes
1999	Ferrari

* The constructors' title has only been awarded since 1958.

CONSTRUCTORS' WORLD CHAMPIONSHIP

	Australia	Brazil	San Marino	Monaco	Spain	Canada	France	Britain	Austria	Germany	Hungary	Belgium	Italy	Europe	Malaysia	Japan	Total
1 Ferrari	10	8	10	16	7	4	3	6	10	16	4	3	5	0	16	10	128
2 McLaren-Mercedes	–	10	6	4	16	10	6	10	10	2	16	16	2	2	4	10	124
3 Jordan-Mugen-Honda	6	4	3	3	0	0	10	5	3	4	4	5	10	–	1	3	61
4 Stewart-Ford	2	–	4	0	–	2	4	0	0	0	2	0	3	14	5	0	36
5 Williams-Supertec	4	3	0	0	2	3	3	4	–	3	0	2	6	3	0	0	35
6 Benetton-Playlife	3	0	2	3	0	6	–	0	2	0	0	0	–	–	0	0	16
7 Prost-Peugeot	–	1	–	0	1	0	0	0	0	1	0	0	0	6	–	–	9
8 Sauber-Petronas	–	–	1	–	–	1	–	1	1	0	0	0	0	–	0	1	5
9 Arrows	1	0	–	–	0	–	0	0	–	–	0	–	–	–	–	0	1
=Minardi-Ford	–	0	0	–	–	0	0	0	0	0	0	0	0	–	1	0	1
NP BAR-Supertec	–	–	0	–	0	–	0	–	0	–	0	0	0	0	–	0	0

NP = no placing   0 = classified but no world championship points gained   – = retired or did not start
Points for constructors: first place: 10 points; second place: 6 points; third place: 4 points; fourth place: 3 points; fifth place: 2 points; sixth place: 1 point.

The Statistics

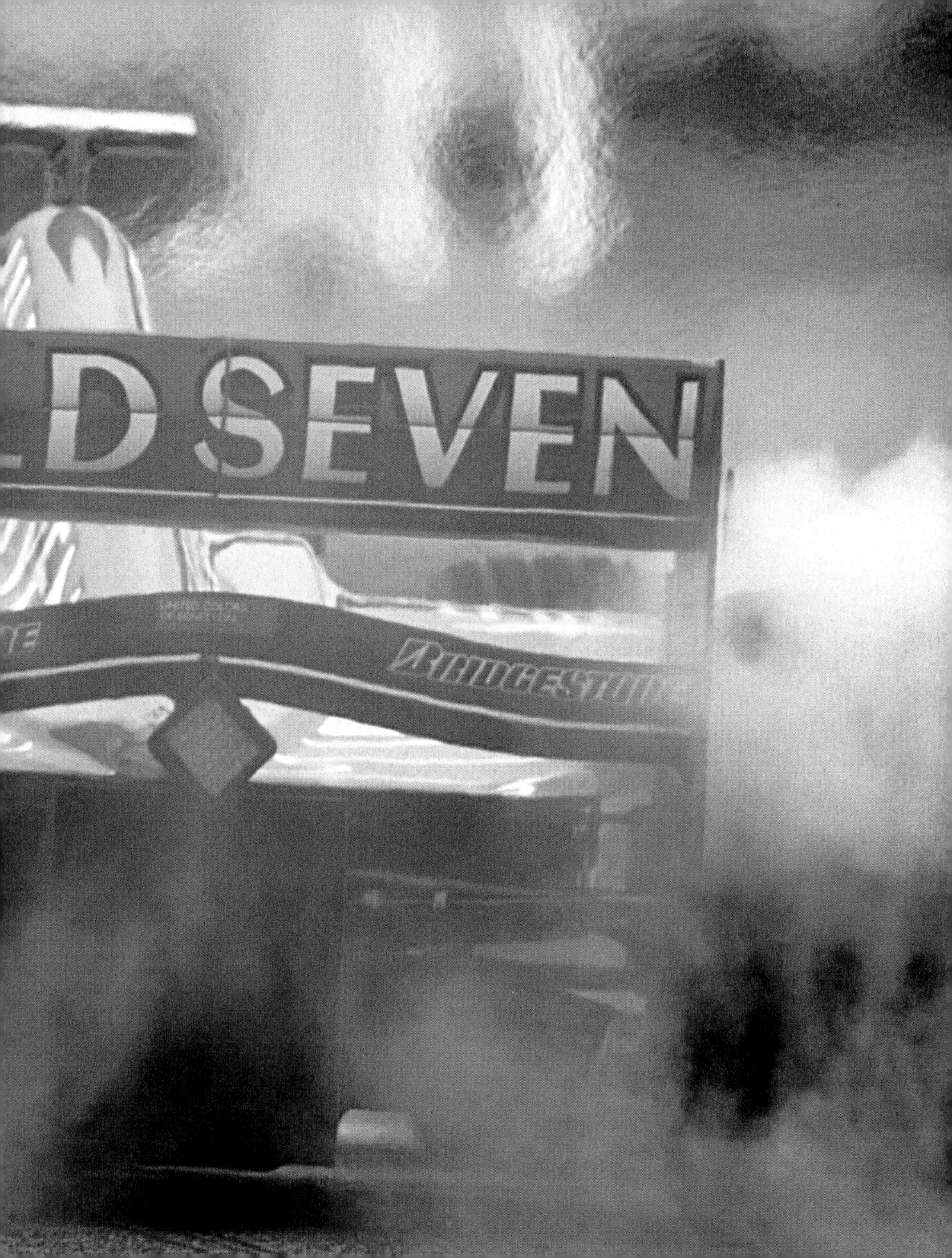
SEVEN

Australian Grand Prix
7 March, Melbourne

Track length: 5.303 km (3.295 miles) • Race distance: 57 laps • Lap record: 1:30.585 min (210.710 kmh/130.929 mph), Heinz-Harald Frentzen, Williams-Renault, 1997 • Fastest lap: Michael Schumacher: 1:32.112 min (207.250 kmh/128.783 mph) • Weather: warm with light cloud cover • Spectators: 103,000

R A C E   R E S U L T S

	Driver	Team	Laps	Time (hours)	Ave. (mph)	Difference
1	Irvine	Ferrari	57	1:35:01.659	118.590	
2	Frentzen	Jordan-Mugen-Honda	57	1:35:02.686	118.569	1.027 sec
3	R. Schumacher	Williams-Supertec	57	1:35:08.671	118.445	5.985 sec
4	Fisichella	Benetton-Playlife	57	1:35:35.077	117.889	26.406 sec
5	Barrichello	Stewart-Ford	57	1:35:56.357	117.463	21.28 sec
6	De la Rosa	Arrows	57	1:36:25.976	116.862	29.619 sec
7	Takagi	Arrows	57	1:36:27.947	116.822	1.971 sec
8	M. Schumacher	Ferrari	56	1:35:16.505	116.207	1 lap

R E T I R E M E N T S

Driver	Team	Lap	Reason	Ave. (mph)
Zonta	BAR-Supertec	48	Engine failure	115.162
Badoer	Minardi-Ford	42	Unknown	113.933
Wurz	Benetton-Playlife	28	Suspension failure	111.439
Diniz	Sauber-Petronas	27	Gearbox failure	112..220
Gené	Minardi-Ford	25	Accident	111.370
Trulli	Prost-Peugeot	25	Accident	111.347
Panis	Prost-Peugeot	23	Unknown	115.471
Hakkinen	McLaren-Mercedes	21	Throttle link failure	108.865
Zanardi	Williams-Supertec	20	Accident	115.970
Coulthard	McLaren-Mercedes	13	Unknown	125.045
Villeneuve	BAR-Supertec	13	Rear-wing failure	122.363
Hill	Jordan-Mugen-Honda	0	Accident	–
Alesi	Sauber-Petronas	0	Stalled	–

Herbert (Stewart-Ford) did not make race restart due to engine failure.

P I T - S T O P S

Lap		Duration* (sec)	Lap		Duration* (sec)
13	Zanardi	.23.512	31	Barrichello	.26.345
15	Diniz	.24.711	31	Zonta	.29.441
15	Zonta	.34.918	32	Takagi	.27.046
15	Badoer	.46.637	32	Barrichello	.26.335
18	Fisichella	.37.052	33	R. Schumacher	.24.890
18	Hakkinen	.47.557	33	Badoer	.27.282
22	Trulli	.23.752	34	Irvine	.24.474
22	Barrichello	.25.027	34	Frentzen	.24.630
22	De la Rosa	.23.919	37	Fisichella	.25.520
23	Gené	.27.215	37	M. Schumacher**	.11.371
23	Trulli	.28.602	38	M. Schumacher	.46.248
27	Wurz	.27.315	40	De la Rosa	.23.293
27	M. Schumacher	.41.287	46	Zonta	.28.728

* Including driving to and from pit   ** Fastest pit-stop

Brazilian Grand Prix
11 April, São Paulo

Track length: 4.292 km (2.667 miles) • Race distance: 72 laps • Lap record: 1:18.397 min (197.089 kmh/122.465 mph), Jacques Villeneuve, Williams-Renault, 1997 • Fastest lap: Mika Hakkinen: 1:18.488 min (196.961 kmh/122.389 mph) • Weather: sunny and hot • Spectators: 119,000

R A C E   R E S U L T S

	Driver	Team	Laps	Time (hours)	Ave. (mph)	Difference
1	Hakkinen	McLaren-Mercedes	72	1:38.03.765	119.921	
2	M. Schumacher	Ferrari	72	1:38.08.710	119.818	4.925 sec
3	Frentzen*	Jordan-Mugen-Honda	71	1:35.58.877	118.459	DNF
4	R. Schumacher	Williams-Supertec	71	1:36.22.860	117.865	1 lap
5	Irvine	Ferrari	71	1:36.23.103	117.984	1 lap
6	Panis	Prost-Peugeot	71	1:37.13.388	116.845	1 lap
7	Wurz	Benetton-Playlife	70	1:36:12.021	116.386	2 laps
8	Takagi	Arrows	69	1:36.10.072	114.798	3 laps
9	Gené	Minardi-Ford	69	1:37.02.116	113.772	3 laps

* Retired but still assessed because of the distance travelled.

R E T I R E M E N T S

Driver	Team	Lap	Reason	Ave. (mph)
De la Rosa	Arrows	52	Hydraulics failure	115.132
Villeneuve	BAR-Supertec	49	Hydraulics failure	115.021
Zanardi	Williams-Supertec	43	Differential failure	111.790
Barrichello	Stewart-Ford	42	Engine failure	112.375
Diniz	Sauber-Petronas	42	Accident	116.738
Fisichella	Benetton-Playlife	38	Clutch failure	117.631
Sarrazin	Minardi-Ford	31	Accident	115.776
Alesi	Sauber-Petronas	27	Gearbox failure	115.952
Coulthard	McLaren-Mercedes	22	Gearbox failure	102.452
Trulli	Prost-Peugeot	21	Gearbox failure	110.696
Herbert	Stewart-Ford	15	Hydraulics failure	116.897
Hill	Jordan-Mugen-Honda	10	Steering failure	111.938

Zonta (BAR-Supertec) did not start.

P I T - S T O P S

Lap		Duration* (sec)	Lap		Duration* (sec)
11	Zanardi	.34.893	40	De la Rosa	.32.772
12	Panis	.34.096	42	Hakkinen	.30.983
20	Trulli	.47.618	41	Wurz	.32.543
22	Coulthard	.33.328	41	Takagi	.32.359
26	Alesi	.46.641	42	Zanardi	.42.514
27	Barrichello	.31.245	43	Villeneuve	.35.085
27	Panis	.37.500	45	Frentzen**	.30.780
34	Gené	.35.674	47	Panis	.31.159
35	R. Schumacher	.33.386	50	Gené	.40.903
38	M. Schumacher	.32.552	55	Irvine	.32.791
40	Irvine	.33.656			

* Including driving to and from pit   ** Fastest pit-stop

San Marino Grand Prix
2 May, Imola

Track length: 4.929 km (3.063 miles) • Race distance: 62 laps • Lap record: 1:25.531 min (207.503 kmh/128.936 mph), Heinz-Harald Frentzen, Williams-Renault, 1997 • Fastest lap: Michael Schumacher: 1:28.547 min (200.43 kmh/124.545 mph) • Weather: sunny • Spectators: 182,000

RACE RESULTS

	Driver	Team	Laps	Time (hours)	Ave. (mph)	Difference
1	M. Schumacher	Ferrari	62	1:33.44.792	121.466	
2	Coulthard	McLaren-Mercedes	62	1:33.49.057	121.374	4.265 sec
3	Barrichello	Stewart-Ford	61	1:33.46.721	119.464	1 lap
4	Hill	Jordan-Mugen-Honda	61	1:33.47.629	119.445	1 lap
5	Fisichella	Benetton-Playlife	61	1:34.27.002	118.615	1 lap
6	Alesi	Sauber-Petronas	61	1:34.33.056	118.489	1 lap
7	Salo*	BAR-Supertec	59	1:32.08.096	117.604	DNF
8	Badoer	Minardi-Ford	59	1:33.53.344	115.409	3 laps
9	Gené	Minardi-Ford	59	1:34.16.112	114.944	3 laps
10	Herbert*	Stewart-Ford	58	1:29.37.619	118.846	DNF
11	Zanardi*	Williams-Supertec	58	1:29.45.043	118.683	DNF

* Retired but still assessed because of the distance travelled.

RETIREMENTS

Driver	Team	Lap	Reason	Ave. (mph)
Diniz	Sauber-Petronas	49	Spun off	112.642
Panis	Prost-Peugeot	48	Engine failure	116.082
Irvine	Ferrari	46	Engine failure	120.722
Frentzen	Jordan-Mugen-Honda	46	Spun off	119.887
Takagi	Arrows	29	Hydraulics failure	115.017
R. Schumacher	Williams-Supertec	28	Engine failure	119.845
Hakkinen	McLaren-Mercedes	17	Accident	122.522
De la Rosa	Arrows	5	Accident	113.602
Wurz	Benetton-Playlife	5	Accident	113.431
Trulli	Prost-Peugeot	0	Accident	—
Villeneuve	BAR-Supertec	0	Gearbox failure	—

PIT-STOPS

Lap		Duration* (sec)	Lap		Duration* (sec)
15	Alesi	27.592	31	M. Schumacher**	23.922
17	Takagi	44.670	31	Herbert	30.613
21	Badoer	26.696	35	Coulthard	26.216
24	Barrichello	26.368	35	Fisichella	28.783
23	Takagi	1:11.604	35	Diniz	3:09.684
23	Gené	28.102	41	Panis	55.569
24	Salo	27.599	41	Gené	25.865
25	Diniz	29.834	40	Diniz	26.956
26	Panis	25.605	43	Barrichello	25.868
27	Frentzen	25.181	42	Badoer	26.644
28	R. Schumacher	26.007	45	M. Schumacher	24.541
29	Irvine	25.237	45	Alesi	25.330
29	Hill	25.640	45	Salo	26.048
29	Zanardi	25.406	46	Zanardi	25.293
30	Alesi	25.879	49	Hill	24.360

* Including driving to and from pit   ** Fastest pit-stop

Monaco Grand Prix
16 May, Monte Carlo

Track length: 3.366 km (2.092 miles) • Race distance: 78 laps • Old lap record: 1:22.948 min (146.13 kmh/90.801mph), Mika Hakkinen, McLaren-Mercedes, 1998 • New lap record: Mika Hakkinen: 1:22.259 (147.35 kmh/91.562 mph) • Weather: sunny • Spectators: 120,000

RACE RESULTS

	Driver	Team	Laps	Time (hours)	Ave. (mph)	Difference
1	M. Schumacher	Ferrari	78	1:49:31.812	89.393	
2	Irvine	Ferrari	78	1:50.02.288	88.980	30.476 sec
3	Hakkinen	McLaren-Mercedes	78	1:50.09.295	88.887	37.483 sec
4	Frentzen	Jordan-Mugen-Honda	78	1:50:25.821	88.665	54.009 sec
5	Fisichella	Benetton-Playlife	77	1:49.32.705	88.235	1 lap
6	Wurz	Benetton-Playlife	77	1:49.47.799	88.033	1 lap
7	Trulli	Prost-Peugeot	77	1:50.05.845	87.792	1 lap
8	Zanardi	Williams-Supertec	76	1:49.49.514	86.867	2 laps
9	Barrichello*	Stewart-Ford	71	1:40.57.711	88.276	DNF

* Retired but still assessed because of the distance travelled.

RETIREMENTS

Driver	Team	Lap	Reason	Ave. (mph)
R. Schumacher	Williams-Supertec	54	Accident	86.174
Alesi	Sauber-Petronas	50	Accident	86.374
Diniz	Sauber-Petronas	49	Accident	87.498
Panis	Prost-Peugeot	40	Engine failure	86.088
Coulthard	McLaren-Mercedes	36	Oil leak	88.491
Salo	BAR-Supertec	36	Brake failure	86.602
Takagi	Arrows	36	Engine failure	85.215
Villeneuve	BAR-Supertec	32	Oil leak	87.855
Herbert	Stewart-Ford	32	Suspension failure	86.739
De la Rosa	Arrows	30	Gearbox failure	83.942
Gené	Minardi-Ford	24	Accident	83.938
Badoer	Minardi-Ford	10	Gearbox failure	82.403
Hill	Jordan-Mugen-Honda	3	Accident	80.128

PIT-STOPS

Lap		Duration* (sec)	Lap		Duration* (sec)
23	Trulli	24.101	50	Barrichello	25.866
27	Panis	23.976	50	Alesi	34.261
37	Irvine	23.387	50	Zanardi	25.839
42	M. Schumacher	26.745	52	Trulli	23.525
43	Fisichella	27.197	52	R. Schumacher	25.357
44	Wurz	26.866	56	Irvine**	23.332
49	Alesi	25.218	57	Frentzen	24.073
50	Hakkinen	26.172			

* Including driving to and from pit   ** Fastest pit-stop

Spanish Grand Prix
30 May, Barcelona

Track length: 4.728 km (2.938 miles) • Race distance: 65 laps • Lap record: 1:22.242 min (206.960 kmh/128.599 mph), Giancarlo Fisichella, Jordan-Peugeot, 1997 • Fastest lap: Michael Schumacher: 1:24.982 min (200.282 kmh/124.453 mph) • Weather: sunny and hot • Spectators: 161,000

RACE RESULTS

	Driver	Team	Laps	Time (hours)	Ave. (mph)	Difference
1	Hakkinen	McLaren-Mercedes	65	1:34:13.665	121.545	
2	Coulthard	McLaren-Mercedes	65	1:34:19.903	121.412	6.238 sec
3	M. Schumacher	Ferrari	65	1:34:24.510	121.313	10.845 sec
4	Irvine	Ferrari	65	1:34:43.847	120.900	30.182 sec
5	R. Schumacher	Williams-Supertec	65	1:35:40.873	119.699	87.208 sec
6	Trulli	Prost-Peugeot	64	1:34:24.028	119.456	1 lap
7	Hill	Jordan-Mugen-Honda	64	1:34:25.044	119.434	1 lap
8	Salo	BAR-Supertec	64	1:35:21.065	118.265	1 lap
9	Fisichella	Benetton-Playlife	64	1:35:22.704	118.231	1 lap
10	Wurz	Benetton-Playlife	64	1:35:29.548	118.090	1 lap
11	De la Rosa	Arrows	63	1:34:41.268	117.232	2 laps
12	Takagi	Arrows	62	1:34:38.929	115.417	3 laps

RETIREMENTS

Driver	Team	Lap	Reason	Ave. (mph)
Badoer	Minardi-Ford	50	Spun off	115.204
Villeneuve	BAR-Supertec	40	Gearbox failure	120.164
Diniz	Sauber-Petronas	40	Gearbox failure	119.611
Herbert	Stewart-Ford	40	Transmission failure	118.442
Frentzen	Jordan-Mugen-Honda	35	Differential failure	119.533
Alesi	Sauber-Petronas	27	Electrical failure	119.419
Zanardi	Williams-Supertec	24	Gearbox failure	118.965
Panis	Prost-Peugeot	24	Oil pressure failure	112.633
Gené	Minardi-Ford	0	Gearbox failure	—
Barrichello	Stewart-Ford	—	Excluded (from 8th position)	—

PIT-STOPS

Lap		Duration* (sec)	Lap		Duration* (sec)
17	De la Rosa	31.842	27	Diniz	25.445
18	Herbert	29.667	31	De la Rosa	27.442
19	Wurz	29.812	33	Wurz**	24.678
19	Badoer	26.909	35	Fisichella	26.312
21	Fisichella	25.310	41	Irvine	26.549
21	Salo	29.344	40	Badoer	32.096
22	Irvine	25.800	42	Trulli	26.149
23	Hakkinen	25.955	41	Takagi	29.493
23	Trulli	26.086	43	M. Schumacher	26.125
23	Takagi	28.299	43	Barrichello	27.605
24	Villeneuve	27.891	44	Hakkinen	26.307
24	M. Schumacher	25.598	44	R. Schumacher	25.374
25	Hill	27.178	45	Coulthard	25.650
26	Coulthard	30.416	46	De la Rosa	30.970
26	Alesi	26.643	48	Fisichella	25.009
26	Frentzen	26.344	49	Wurz	25.587
26	Barrichello	26.947	50	Hill	25.455
27	R. Schumacher	26.764	50	Salo	26.161

* Including driving to and from pit   ** Fastest pit-stop

Canadian Grand Prix
13 June, Montreal

Track length: 4.421 km (2.747 miles) • Race distance: 69 laps • Lap record: 1:19.379 min (200.501 kmh/124.586 mph), Michael Schumacher, Ferrari, 1998 • Fastest lap: Eddie Irvine, 1:20.382 (197.994 kmh/123.031 mph) • Weather: sunny and very hot • Spectators: 262,244

RACE RESULTS

	Driver	Team	Laps	Time (hours)	Ave. (mph)	Difference
1	Hakkinen	McLaren-Mercedes	69	1:41.35.727	111.943	
2	Fisichella	Benetton-Playlife	69	1:41.36.509	111.929	0.781 sec
3	Irvine	Ferrari	69	1:41.37.524	111.910	1.798 sec
4	R. Schumacher	Williams-Supertec	69	1:41.38.119	111.899	2.391 sec
5	Herbert	Stewart-Ford	69	1:41.38.532	111.892	2.804 sec
6	Diniz	Sauber-Petronas	69	1:41.39.438	111.875	3.710 sec
7	Coulthard	McLaren-Mercedes	69	1:41.40.731	111.851	5.003 sec
8	Gené	Minardi-Ford	68	1:41.39.918	110.245	1 lap
9	Panis	Prost-Peugeot	68	1:41.40.658	110.231	1 lap
10	Badoer	Minardi-Ford	67	1:41.38.062	108.657	2 laps
11	Frentzen*	Jordan-Mugen-Honda	65	1:34.50.784	112.957	DNF

* Retired but still assessed because of the distance travelled

RETIREMENTS

Driver	Team	Lap	Reason	Ave. (mph)
Zanardi	Williams-Supertec	50	Spun off	109.732
Takagi	Arrows	41	Transmission failure	108.882
Villeneuve	BAR-Supertec	34	Accident	110.530
M. Schumacher	Ferrari	29	Accident	111.186
De la Rosa	Arrows	22	Transmission failure	105.961
Hill	Jordan-Mugen-Honda	14	Accident	100.102
Barrichello	Stewart-Ford	14	Body damage	93.678
Zonta	BAR-Supertec	2	Accident	87.966
Alesi	Sauber-Petronas	0	Accident	—
Trulli	Prost-Peugeot	0	Accident	—
Wurz	Benetton-Playlife	0	Accident	—

PIT-STOPS

Lap		Duration* (sec)	Lap		Duration* (sec)
1	Barrichello	2:58.079	37	Irvine	29.317
24	Herbert	26.526	36	Panis**	25.716
28	Takagi	26.514	36	Gené	39.525
36	Fisichella	26.762	37	Zanardi	28.150
36	Frentzen	25.746	38	Coulthard	27.916
36	Diniz	28.924	41	Coulthard	30.812
36	R. Schumacher	28.450	46	Badoer	27.260
36	Herbert	32.728	48	Zanardi	26.890
37	Hakkinen	26.079	49	Coulthard	28.305
36	Badoer	29.452	49	Panis	27.530

* Including driving to and from pit   ** Fastest pit-stop

French Grand Prix
27 June, Magny Cours

Track length: 4.247 km (2.639 miles) • Race distance: 72 laps • Lap record: 1:17.070 min (198.521 kmh/123.355 mph), Nigel Mansell, Williams-Renault, 1992 • Fastest lap: David Coulthard: 1:19.227 min (193.109 kmh/119.996 mph) • Weather: dry then wet • Spectators: 205,000

R A C E   R E S U L T S

	Driver	Team	Laps	Time (hours)	Ave. (mph)	Difference
1	Frentzen	Jordan-Mugen-Honda	72	1:58.24.343	96.303	
2	Hakkinen	McLaren-Mercedes	72	1:58.35.435	96.141	11.092 sec
3	Barrichello	Stewart-Ford	72	1:59.07.775	95.706	43.432 sec
4	R. Schumacher	Williams-Supertec	72	1:59.09.818	95.679	45.475 sec
5	M. Schumacher	Ferrari	72	1:59.12.224	95.646	47.881 sec
6	Irvine	Ferrari	72	1:59.13.244	95.633	48.901 sec
7	Trulli	Prost-Peugeot	72	1:59.22.114	95.514	57.771 sec
8	Panis	Prost-Peugeot	72	1:59.22.874	95.504	58.531 sec
9	Zonta	BAR-Supertec	72	1:59.53.107	95.103	88.764 sec
10	Badoer	Minardi-Ford	71	1:59.05.221	94.409	1 lap
11	De la Rosa	Arrows	71	1:59.53.956	93.835	1 lap

R E T I R E M E N T S

Driver	Team	Lap	Reason	Ave. (mph)
Fisichella	Benetton-Playlife	42	Spun off	92.507
Hill	Jordan-Mugen-Honda	31	Electrical failure	87.866
Zanardi	Williams-Supertec	26	Spun off	104.457
Villeneuve	BAR-Supertec	25	Spun off	108.210
Wurz	Benetton-Playlife	25	Spun off	106.954
Gené	Minardi-Ford	25	Spun off	105.555
Alesi	Sauber-Petronas	24	Spun off	111.478
Coulthard	McLaren-Mercedes	9	Engine failure	117.384
Diniz	Sauber-Petronas	5	Driveshaft failure	112.287
Herbert	Stewart-Ford	4	Gearbox failure	102.296

Takagi (Arrows) was disqualified (from 11th place) for use of illegal tyres.

P I T - S T O P S

Lap		Duration* (sec)	Lap		Duration* (sec)
21	Panis	27.102	22	Zonta	32.892
21	Irvine	1:03.796	22	Zanardi	34.142
21	Fisichella	33.768	22	Badoer	30.794
21	Wurz	55.787	22	Hill	49.730
21	Villeneuve	31.957	25	Villeneuve	28.289
21	Hill	46.939	28	Takagi	36.014
21	De la Rosa	32.181	50	Irvine	25.461
21	Takagi	1:00.845	52	R. Schumacher	25.943
21	Gené	31.260	54	M. Schumacher	31.627
22	Barrichello	31.067	57	Panis	24.974
22	Hakkinen	28.769	59	Trulli	24.315
22	Alesi	30.292	60	De la Rosa	32.798
22	Frentzen	32.800	61	Zonta	30.411
22	M. Schumacher	27.946	65	Hakkinen	25.480
22	R. Schumacher	32.593	65	Barrichello	25.993
22	Trulli	27.465	67	Badoer**	23.462

* Including driving to and from pit   ** Fastest pit-stop

British Grand Prix
11 July, Silverstone

Track length: 5.137 km (3.192 miles) • Race distance: 60 laps • Lap record: 1:24.475 min (219.047 kmh/136.109 mph), Michael Schumacher, Ferrari, 1997 • Fastest lap: Mika Hakkinen: 1:28.309 (209.53 kmh/130.2 mph) • Weather: sunny • Spectators: 245,000

R A C E   R E S U L T S

	Driver	Team	Laps	Time (hours)	Ave. (mph)	Difference
1	Coulthard	McLaren-Mercedes	60	1:32:30.144	124.256	
2	Irvine	Ferrari	60	1:32:31.973	124.215	1.829 sec
3	R. Schumacher	Williams-Supertec	60	1:32:57.555	123.645	27.411 sec
4	Frentzen	Jordan-Mugen-Honda	60	1:32:57.933	123.637	27.789 sec
5	Hill	Jordan-Mugen-Honda	60	1:33:08.750	123.397	38.606 sec
6	Diniz	Sauber-Petronas	60	1:33:23.787	123.066	53.643 sec
7	Fisichella	Benetton-Playlife	60	1:33:24.758	123.045	54.614 sec
8	Barrichello	Stewart-Ford	60	1:33:38.734	122.739	68.590 sec
9	Trulli	Prost-Peugeot	60	1:33:42.189	122.664	72.045 sec
10	Wurz	Benetton-Playlife	60	1:33:42.267	122.662	72.123 sec
11	Zanardi	Williams-Supertec	60	1:33:47.268	122.552	77.124 sec
12	Herbert	Stewart-Ford	60	1:33:47.853	122.540	77.709 sec
13	Panis	Prost-Peugeot	60	1:33:50.636	122.479	80.492 sec
14	Alesi	Sauber-Petronas	59	1:33:12.794	121.253	1 lap
15	Gené	Minardi-Ford	58	1:32:41.812	119.861	2 laps
16	Takagi	Arrows	58	1:33:15.047	119.149	2 laps

R E T I R E M E N T S

Driver	Team	Lap	Reason	Ave. (mph)
Zonta	BAR-Supertec	41	Suspension failure	120.227
Hakkinen	McLaren-Mercedes	35	Wheel hub failure	118.325
Villeneuve	BAR-Supertec	29	Gearbox failure	121.891
Badoer	Minardi-Ford	6	Gearbox failure	108.882
De la Rosa	Arrows	0	Gearbox failure	—

M. Schumacher (Ferrari) did not make restart due to accident.

P I T - S T O P S

Lap		Duration* (sec)	Lap		Duration* (sec)
6	Badoer	1:16.216	31	Trulli	27.606
19	Gené	27.733	31	Zonta	29.855
20	Fisichella	26.888	33	Alesi	32.397
20	Takagi	27.446	34	Alesi	43.003
21	Alesi	27.134	38	Panis	27.253
21	Wurz	27.306	39	Zanardi	28.324
22	Zanardi	26.277	40	R. Schumacher	28.977
23	Hill	27.912	40	Herbert	27.271
23	Herbert	25.790	41	Irvine	26.084
24	Coulthard	26.351	41	Diniz	28.095
24	Frentzen	28.993	41	Wurz	27.017
24	R. Schumacher	26.294	40	Gené	26.854
24	Diniz	27.098	42	Zonta	28.716
24	Trulli	26.098	42	Coulthard	25.275
25	Hakkinen	28.118	42	Barrichello	27.399
25	Barrichello	28.178	42	Fisichella	27.202
25	Zonta	26.603	41	Takagi	31.186
26	Irvine	30.644	45	Frentzen	25.333
26	Hakkinen	47.874	46	Hill**	25.162
26	Panis	26.391	47	Barrichello	28.595
29	Villeneuve	30.877	49	Herbert	31.021
29	Hakkinen	58.018			

* Including driving to and from pit   ** Fastest pit-stop

Austrian Grand Prix
25 July, A-1 Ring

Track length: 4.319 km (2.684 miles) • Race distance: 71 laps • Lap record: 1:11.814 min (216.709 kmh/134.657 mph), Jacques Villeneuve, Williams-Renault, 1997 • Fastest lap: Mika Hakkinen: 1:12.107 min (207.250 kmh/133.986 mph) • Weather: warm with cloud cover • Spectators: 136,000

RACE RESULTS

	Driver	Team	Laps	Time (hours)	Ave. (mph)	Difference
1	Irvine	Ferrari	71	1:28:12.438	129.610	
2	Coulthard	McLaren-Mercedes	71	1:28:12.751	129.602	0.313 sec
3	Hakkinen	McLaren-Mercedes	71	1:28:34.720	129.066	22.282 sec
4	Frentzen	Jordan-Mugen-Honda	71	1:29:05.241	128.329	52.803 sec
5	Wurz	Benetton-Playlife	71	1:29:18.796	128.005	66.358 sec
6	Diniz	Sauber-Petronas	71	1:29:23.371	127.896	70.933 sec
7	Trulli	Prost-Peugeot	70	1:28:28.541	127.397	1 lap
8	Hill	Jordan-Mugen-Honda	70	1:28:29.690	127.369	1 lap
9	Salo	Ferrari	70	1:28:35.747	127.224	1 lap
10	Panis	Prost-Peugeot	70	1:28:40.035	127.121	1 lap
11	Gené	Minardi-Ford	70	1:29:25.126	126.053	1 lap
12	Fisichella*	Benetton-Playlife	68	1:25:51.478	127.530	DNF
13	Badoer	Minardi-Ford	68	1:28:58.188	123.069	3 laps
14	Herbert	Stewart-Ford	67	1:29:20.589	120.753	4 laps
15	Zonta*	BAR-Supertec	63	1:19:59.481	126.818	DNF

* Retired but still assessed because of the distance travelled

RETIREMENTS

Driver	Team	Lap	Reason	Ave. (mph)
Barrichello	Stewart-Ford	55	Engine failure	128.332
Alesi	Sauber-Petronas	49	Out of fuel	127.810
De la Rosa	Arrows	38	Spun out	124.609
Zanardi	Williams-Supertec	35	Out of fuel	126.246
Villeneuve	BAR-Supertec	34	Driveshaft failure	126.310
Takagi	Arrows	25	Engine failure	125.243
R. Schumacher	Williams-Supertec	8	Spun out	123.091

PIT-STOPS

Lap		Duration* (sec)	Lap		Duration* (sec)
1	Herbert	5:08.686	40	Hakkinen	27.429
2	Badoer	41.011	41	Salo	26.754
3	Salo	37.716	39	Herbert	28.512
20	Badoer	28.890	43	Fisichella	28.412
24	Diniz	27.706	44	Irvine	26.545
25	Alesi	26.127	44	Frentzen	26.611
30	De la Rosa	31.683	44	Wurz	27.225
35	Gené	30.547	45	Trulli	26.150
38	Barrichello	30.620	45	Hill	27.389
26	Badoer	34.606	46	Panis	25.921
38	Zonta	29.764	52	Diniz**	24.802
39	Coulthard	28.174			

* Including driving to and from pit   ** Fastest pit-stop

German Grand Prix
1 August, Hockenheim

Track length: 6.822 km (4.239 miles) • Race distance: 45 laps • Old lap record: 1:46.211 min (234.144 kmh/143.630 mph), David Coulthard, Williams-Renault, 1994 • New lap record: David Coulthard: 1:45.270 min (233.324 kmh/144.985 mph) • Weather: sunny and very hot • Spectators: 237,000

RACE RESULTS

	Driver	Team	Laps	Time (hours)	Ave. (mph)	Difference
1	Irvine	Ferrari	45	1:21.58.594	139.636	
2	Salo	Ferrari	45	1:21.59.601	139.608	1.007 sec
3	Frentzen	Jordan-Mugen-Honda	45	1:22.03.789	139.489	5.195 sec
4	R. Schumacher	Williams-Supertec	45	1:22.11.403	139.274	12.809 sec
5	Coulthard	McLaren-Mercedes	45	1:22.15.417	139.160	16.823 sec
6	Panis	Prost-Peugeot	45	1:22.28.473	138.794	29.879 sec
7	Wurz	Benetton-Playlife	45	1:22.31.927	138.697	33.333 sec
8	Alesi	Sauber-Petronas	45	1:23.09.885	137.642	71.291 sec
9	Gené	Minardi-Ford	45	1:23.46.912	136.628	108.318 sec
10	Badoer	Minardi-Ford	44	1:22.14.172	136.103	1 lap
11	Herbert*	Stewart-Ford	40	1:13.24.080	138.622	DNF

* Retired but still assessed because of the distance travelled.

RETIREMENTS

Driver	Team	Lap	Reason	Ave. (mph)
De la Rosa	Arrows	37	Accident	136.198
Hakkinen	McLaren-Mercedes	25	Accident	139.154
Zanardi	Williams-Supertec	21	Differential failure	136.161
Zonta	BAR-Supertec	20	Engine failure	135.568
Takagi	Arrows	15	Engine failure	135.811
Hill	Jordan-Mugen-Honda	13	Brakes failure	136.997
Trulli	Prost-Peugeot	10	Engine failure	137.350
Fisichella	Benetton-Playlife	7	Suspension failure	132.070
Barrichello	Stewart-Ford	6	Hydraulics failure	130.820
Villeneuve	BAR-Supertec	0	Accident	—
Diniz	Sauber-Petronas	0	Accident	—

PIT-STOPS

Lap		Duration* (sec)	Lap		Duration* (sec)
1	Alesi	29.324	22	Badoer	29.538
3	Fisichella	36.599	23	Salo	28.013
10	Coulthard	32.399	23	Herbert	29.557
15	Zonta	41.028	23	Wurz	27.123
16	Alesi	25.796	24	Hakkinen	42.414
18	Panis	26.089	24	R.Schumacher	27.704
20	Gené	30.279	26	Coulthard	28.022
21	Frentzen	28.919	28	Alesi	26.636
21	De la Rosa	31.350	30	Panis	26.567
22	Irvine	27.362	39	Coulthard**	25.168

* Including driving to and from pit   ** Fastest pit-stop

Hungarian Grand Prix
15 August, Hungaroring

Track length: 3.972 km (2.468 miles) • Race distance: 77 laps • Lap record: 1:18.308 min (182.418 kmh/113.349 mph), Nigel Mansell, Williams-Renault, 1992 • Fastest lap: David Coulthard: 1:20.699 min (177.230 kmh/110.129 mph) • Weather: sunny • Spectators: 250,000

RACE RESULTS

	Driver	Team	Laps	Time (hours)	Ave. (mph)	Difference
1	Hakkinen	McLaren-Mercedes	77	1:46.23.536	107.201	
2	Coulthard	McLaren-Mercedes	77	1:46.33.242	107.039	9.706 sec
3	Irvine	Ferrari	77	1:46.50.764	106.746	27.228 sec
4	Frentzen	Jordan-Mugen-Honda	77	1:46.55.351	106.670	31.815 sec
5	Barrichello	Stewart-Ford	77	1:47.07.344	106.471	43.808 sec
6	Hill	Jordan-Mugen-Honda	77	1:47.19.282	106.274	55.726 sec
7	Wurz	Benetton-Playlife	77	1:47.24.548	106.187	61.012 sec
8	Trulli	Prost-Peugeot	76	1:46.44.214	105.467	1 lap
9	R. Schumacher	Williams-Supertec	76	1:46.53.291	105.318	1 lap
10	Panis	Prost-Peugeot	76	1:47.06.627	105.100	1 lap
11	Herbert	Stewart-Ford	76	1:47.29.749	104.723	1 lap
12	Salo	Ferrari	75	1:46.26.728	104.332	2 laps
13	Zonta	BAR-Supertec	75	1:46.29.795	104.315	2 laps
14	Badoer	Minardi-Ford	75	1:46.50.082	103.985	2 laps
15	De la Rosa	Arrows	75	1:46.58.088	103.855	2 laps
16	Alesi*	Sauber-Petronas	74	1:43.41.491	105.708	DNF
17	Gené	Minardi-Ford	74	1:46.66.006	102.503	3 laps

* Retired but still assessed because of the distance travelled.

RETIREMENTS

Driver	Team	Lap	Reason	Ave. (mph)
Villeneuve	BAR-Supertec	60	Clutch failure	104.419
Fisichella	Benetton-Playlife	52	Fuel pressure failure	106.350
Takagi	Arrows	26	Driveshaft failure	100.960
Diniz	Sauber-Petronas	19	Spun out	105.667
Zanardi	Williams-Supertec	10	Differential failure	100.297

PIT-STOPS

Lap		Duration* (sec)	Lap		Duration* (sec)
23	Villeneuve	31.005	38	Panis	32.556
25	Takagi	30.757	40	Barrichello	33.654
28	Fisichella	30.796	44	Salo	31.394
28	R. Schumacher	32.494	48	Hill	31.063
28	De la Rosa	31.412	50	Frentzen	30.213
29	Irvine	30.782	50	Trulli	29.957
29	Hill	33.109	50	Villeneuve	32.393
29	Wurz	30.132	51	Wurz	30.613
29	Trulli	29.468	51	R. Schumacher	29.889
29	Zonta	32.999	51	Badoer	30.681
29	Badoer	30.310	52	De la Rosa	31.660
30	Frentzen	29.146	54	Alesi	46.069
31	Hakkinen	30.002	55	Hakkinen	30.692
32	Alesi	29.850	58	Irvine	28.868
33	Coulthard	29.284	58	Coulthard**	28.593
33	Zonta	31.816	60	Zonta	31.554
33	Gené	35.960	69	Alesi	33.622
38	Herbert	34.625			

* Including driving to and from pit   ** Fastest pit-stop

Belgian Grand Prix
29 August, Spa-Francorchamps

Track length: 6.968 km (4.330 miles) • Race distance: 44 laps • Lap record: 1:51.095 min (225.99 kmh/140.424 mph), Alain Prost, Williams-Renault, 1993 • Fastest lap: Mika Hakkinen: 1:53.955 (220.122 kmh/136.781 mph) • Weather: sunny • Spectators: 168,000

RACE RESULTS

	Driver	Team	Laps	Time (hours)	Ave. (mph)	Difference
1	Coulthard	McLaren-Mercedes	44	1:25.43.057	133.343	
2	Hakkinen	McLaren-Mercedes	44	1:25.53.526	133.072	10.469 sec
3	Frentzen	Jordan-Mugen-Honda	44	1:26.16.490	132.482	33.433 sec
4	Irvine	Ferrari	44	1:26.28.005	132.188	44.948 sec
5	R. Schumacher	Williams-Supertec	44	1:26.31.124	132.108	48.067 sec
6	Hill	Jordan-Mugen-Honda	44	1:26.37.973	131.935	54.916 sec
7	Salo	Ferrari	44	1:26.39.306	131.900	56.249 sec
8	Zanardi	Williams-Supertec	44	1:26.50.079	131.628	67.022 sec
9	Alesi	Sauber-Petronas	44	1:26.56.905	131.455	73.848 sec
10	Barrichello	Stewart-Ford	44	1:27.03.799	131.282	80.742 sec
11	Fisichella	Benetton-Playlife	44	1:27.15.252	130.995	92.195 sec
12	Trulli	Prost-Peugeot	44	1:27.19.211	130.896	96.154 sec
13	Panis	Prost-Peugeot	44	1:27.24.600	130.761	101.543 sec
14	Wurz	Benetton-Playlife	44	1:27.40.802	130.359	117.745 sec
15	Villeneuve	BAR-Supertec	43	1:25.49.704	130.144	1 lap
16	Gené	Minardi-Ford	43	1:26.19.557	129.394	1 lap

RETIREMENTS

Driver	Team	Lap	Reason	Ave. (mph)
De la Rosa	Arrows	35	Transmission failure	127.751
Badoer	Minardi-Ford	33	Suspension failure	128.849
Zonta	BAR-Supertec	33	Gearbox failure	123.137
Herbert	Stewart-Ford	27	Brakes failure	130.179
Diniz	Sauber-Petronas	19	Accident	128.555
Takagi	Arrows	0	Clutch failure	—

PIT-STOPS

Lap		Duration* (sec)	Lap		Duration* (sec)
12	Panis	30.260	22	Wurz	32.561
13	Badoer	32.123	21	Zonta	33.351
14	Alesi	32.343	26	Villeneuve	31.944
14	Trulli	29.281	26	Badoer	31.758
14	Gené	30.399	27	Panis	29.909
14	De la Rosa	30.309	28	Hill	29.480
15	Herbert	32.282	29	Alesi	29.849
15	Diniz	31.008	29	Gené	31.109
16	Hill	28.743	29	De la Rosa	31.700
17	Frentzen	29.533	30	Trulli	28.683
17	Salo	29.990	31	Hakkinen	31.749
17	Barrichello	33.038	31	Zanardi	28.711
18	Hakkinen	29.917	32	Coulthard	28.784
18	Irvine	28.824	32	Frentzen**	28.275
19	Coulthard	29.025	32	Irvine	29.522
21	Zanardi	30.818	32	Barrichello	29.874
21	Fisichella	32.824	34	Salo	28.379
22	R. Schumacher	33.944			

* Including driving to and from pit   ** Fastest pit-stop

Italian Grand Prix
12 September, Monza

Track length: 5.769 km (3.585 miles) • Race distance: 53 laps • Lap record: 1:24.808 min (244.929 kmh/152.192 mph), Mika Hakkinen, McLaren-Mercedes, 1997 • Fastest lap: Ralf Schumacher: 1:25.579 min (241.847 kmh/150.821 mph) • Weather: sunny and very hot • Spectators: 180,000

R A C E   R E S U L T S

	Driver	Team	Laps	Time (hours)	Ave. (mph)	Difference
1	Frentzen	Jordan-Mugen-Honda	53	1:17:02.923	147.848	
2	R. Schumacher	Williams-Supertec	53	1:17:06.195	147.743	3.272 sec
3	Salo	Ferrari	53	1:17:14.855	147.468	11.932 sec
4	Barrichello	Stewart-Ford	53	1:17:20.553	147.286	17.630 sec
5	Coulthard	McLaren-Mercedes	53	1:17:21.085	147.270	18.142 sec
6	Irvine	Ferrari	53	1:17:30.325	146.978	27.402 sec
7	Zanardi	Williams-Supertec	53	1:17:30.970	146.956	28.047 sec
8	Villeneuve	BAR-Supertec	53	1:17:44.720	146.523	41.797 sec
9	Alesi	Sauber-Petronas	53	1:17:45.121	146.511	42.198 sec
10	Hill	Jordan-Mugen-Honda	53	1:17:59.182	146.071	56.259 sec
11	Panis*	Prost-Peugeot	52	1:16:30.578	146.078	DNF

* Retired but still assessed because of the distance travelled.

R E T I R E M E N T S

Driver	Team	Lap	Reason	Ave. (mph)
Herbert	Stewart-Ford	40	Clutch failure	145.574
Takagi	Arrows	35	Spun out	148.555
De la Rosa	Arrows	35	Accidental damage	133.463
Hakkinen	McLaren-Mercedes	29	Spun out	148.119
Trulli	Prost-Peugeot	29	Gearbox failure	143.499
Zonta	BAR-Supertec	25	Wheel bearing failure	142.636
Badoer	Minardi-Ford	23	Accident	142.493
Wurz	Benetton-Playlife	11	Electronics failure	139.971
Diniz	Sauber-Petronas	1	Spun out	123.992
Fisichella	Benetton-Playlife	1	Accident	122.804
Gené	Minardi-Ford	0	Accident	–

P I T - S T O P S

Lap		Duration* (sec)	Lap		Duration* (sec)
1	De la Rosa	2:48.245	33	Alesi	20.781
16	Panis	19.569	34	Hill	22.442
17	Trulli	19.446	31	De la Rosa	21.741
24	Takagi	38.995	35	Frentzen	19.299
25	Zonta	29.057	35	Irvine**	18.961
27	Herbert	25.360	35	Villeneuve	20.931
29	Barrichello	23.128	36	Salo	19.301
32	Panis	20.722	36	Coulthard	20.137
33	R. Schumacher	21.102			

* Including driving to and from pit   ** Fastest pit-stop

European Grand Prix
26 September, Nürburgring

Track length: 4.556 km (2.831 miles) • Race distance: 66 laps • Lap record: 1:18.805 min (208.128 kmh/129.325 mph), Heinz-Harard Frentzen, Williams-Renault, 1997 • Fastest lap: Mika Hakkinen: 1:21.282 min (201.780 kmh/125.384 mph) • Weather: cool with rain in patches • Spectators: 142,000

R A C E   R E S U L T S

	Driver	Team	Laps	Time (hours)	Ave. (mph)	Difference
1	Herbert	Stewart-Ford	66	1:41.54.314	110.004	
2	Trulli	Prost-Peugeot	66	1:42.16.933	109.598	22.618 sec
3	Barrichello	Stewart-Ford	66	1:42.17.180	109.577	22.865 sec
4	R. Schumacher	Williams-Supertec	66	1:42.33.822	109.297	39.507 sec
5	Hakkinen	McLaren-Mercedes	66	1:42.57.264	108.883	62.950 sec
6	Gené	Minardi-Ford	66	1:42.59.468	108.844	65.154 sec
7	Irvine	Ferrari	66	1:43.00.997	108.817	66.683 sec
8	Zonta	BAR-Supertec	65	1:42.08.914	108.079	1 lap
9	Panis	Prost-Peugeot	65	1:42.18.099	107.917	1 lap
10	Villeneuve	BAR-Supertec	61	1:35.55.300	108.012	DNF

* Retired but still assessed because of the distance travelled.

R E T I R E M E N T S

Driver	Team	Lap	Reason	Ave. (mph)
Badoer	Minardi-Ford	53	Gearbox failure	106.925
De la Rosa	Arrows	52	Gearbox failure	103.171
Fisichella	Benetton-Playlife	48	Spun out	107.971
Salo	Ferrari	44	Spun out	102.764
Takagi	Arrows	42	Accident	102.835
Coulthard	McLaren-Mercedes	37	Spun out	109.936
Alesi	Sauber-Petronas	35	Transmission failure	108.095
Frentzen	Jordan-Mugen-Honda	32	Electrical failure	110.082
Zanardi	Williams-Supertec	10	Accident	91.939
Hill	Jordan-Mugen-Honda	0	Electrical failure	–
Wurz	Benetton-Playlife	0	Accident	–
Diniz	Sauber-Petronas	0	Accident	–

P I T - S T O P S

Lap		Duration* (sec)	Lap		Duration* (sec)
12	De la Rosa	30.908	32	Fisichella	25.972
19	Panis	28.712	33	Villeneuve	32.375
19	Zonta	28.855	34	Gené	30.081
19	Takagi	28.478	35	Herbert	33.009
20	Hakkinen	31.727	35	Trulli	27.726
20	Salo	59.290	35	Badoer	57.181
21	Irvine	48.124	35	Alesi	31.224
22	Takagi	26.499	37	Barrichello	32.592
23	Panis	32.793	40	Irvine	28.754
23	Salo	27.533	44	R. Schumacher	29.356
24	Hakkinen	27.484	44	Zonta	29.241
24	Zonta	26.818	44	Panis	27.910
27	R. Schumacher	26.564	47	Herbert	26.922
28	Trulli	27.025	46	De la Rosa	1:09.242
28	Alesi	31.720	48	Trulli	26.646
32	Frentzen	26.050	49	Irvine**	25.726
32	Coulthard	26.816	50	R. Schumacher	33.687

* Including driving to and from pit   ** Fastest pit-stop

Malaysian Grand Prix
17 October, Sepang

Track length: 5.542 km (3.444 miles) • Race distance: 56 laps • Lap record: none (the 1999 Malaysian Grand Prix was the first fixture of the new circuit) • Fastest lap: Heinz-Harald Frentzen: 1:40.631 (191.524 kmh/119.011 mph) • Weather: hot and humid • Spectators: 142,000

R A C E   R E S U L T S

	Driver	Team	Laps	Time (hours)	Ave. (mph)	Difference
1	Irvine*	Ferrari	56	1:36.38.494	119.730	
2	M. Schumacher*	Ferrari	56	1:36.39.534	119.708	1.040 sec
3	Hakkinen	McLaren-Mercedes	56	1:36.48.237	119.526	9.743 sec
4	Herbert	Stewart-Ford	56	1:36.56.032	119.366	17.538 sec
5	Barrichello	Stewart-Ford	56	1:37.10.790	119.064	32.296 sec
6	Frentzen	Jordan-Mugen-Honda	56	1:37.13.378	119.011	34.884 sec
7	Alesi	Sauber-Petronas	56	1:37.32.902	118.614	54.408 sec
8	Wurz	Benetton-Playlife	56	1:37.39.428	118.482	60.934 sec
9	Gené	Minardi-Ford	55	1:37.10.056	116.953	1 lap
10	Zanardi	Williams-Supertec	55	1:37.36.473	116.425	1 lap
11	Fisichella	Benetton-Playlife	52	1:38.14.562	109.363	4 laps

* Disqualified after the race but reinstated on appeal

R E T I R E M E N T S

Driver	Team	Lap	Reason	Ave. (mph)
Villeneuve	BAR-Supertec	48	Hydraulics failure	117.815
Diniz	Sauber-Petronas	44	Spun out	117.905
De la Rosa	Arrows	30	Engine failure	115.617
Badoer	Minardi-Ford	15	Engine overheating	107.289
Coulthard	McLaren-Mercedes	14	Fuel-pressure failure	118.811
R. Schumacher	Williams-Supertec	7	Spun out	114.821
Takagi	Arrows	7	Driveshaft failure	94.110
Zonta	BAR-Supertec	6	Water leak	111.952
Panis	Prost-Peugeot	5	Engine failure	111.872
Hill	Jordan-Mugen-Honda	0	Accident	—
Trulli	Prost-Peugeot	0	Engine failure	—

P I T - S T O P S

Lap		Duration* (sec)	Lap		Duration* (sec)
1	Fisichella	6:50.649	28	M. Schumacher	32.523
3	Zanardi	29.094	28	Herbert	35.081
12	Badoer	35.435	28	Zanardi	32.546
19	Barrichello	30.266	30	Frentzen	30.607
20	Wurz	30.530	38	Wurz	28.755
21	Alesi	30.425	38	Villeneuve	30.817
22	Villeneuve	30.515	39	Barrichello	29.983
22	Diniz	29.695	39	Diniz	28.975
20	Fisichella	29.839	41	Irvine	28.224
24	De la Rosa	32.443	41	Alesi	29.338
25	Irvine	28.899	37	Fisichella	29.249
27	Hakkinen	29.149	47	Hakkinen	28.388
27	Gené	32.624	48	Zanardi**	27.435

* Including driving to and from pit   ** Fastest pit-stop

Japanese Grand Prix
31 October, Suzuka

Track length: 5.864 km (3.644 miles) • Race distance: 53 laps • Lap record: 1:38.942 min (213.355 kmh/132.576 mph), Heinz-Harald Frentzen, Williams-Renault, 1997 • Fastest lap: 1:41.319 (208.355 km/h/129.469 mph), Michael Schumacher, Ferrari • Weather: Dry, sunny • Spectators: 148,000

R A C E   R E S U L T S

	Driver	Team	Laps	Time (hours)	Ave. (mph)	Difference
1	Hakkinen	McLaren-Mercedes	53	1:31.18.785	126.817	
2	M. Schumacher	Ferrari	53	1:31.23.800	126.700	05.015 sec
3	Irvine	Ferrari	53	1:32.54.473	124.640	1:35.688 sec
4	Frentzen	Jordan-Mugen-Honda	53	1:32.57.420	124.574	1:38.635 sec
5	R. Schumacher	Williams-Supertec	53	1:32.58.279	124.555	1:39.494 sec
6	Alesi	Sauber-Petronas	52	1:31.31.101	124.143	1 lap
7	Herbert	Stewart-Ford	52	1:31.33.352	124.092	1 lap
8	Barrichello	Stewart-Ford	52	1:31.34.255	124.072	1 lap
9	Villeneuve	BAR-Supertec	52	1:31.46.116	123.805	1 lap
10	Wurz	Benetton-Supertec	52	1:31.55.310	123.598	1 lap
11	Diniz	Sauber-Petronas	52	1:32.16.261	123.130	1 lap
12	Zonta	BAR-Supertec	52	1:32.44.136	122.513	1 lap
13	De la Rosa	Arrows	51	1:31.39.475	121.569	2 laps

R E T I R E M E N T S

Driver	Team	Lap	Reason	Ave. (mph)
Fisichella	Benetton-Supertec	47	Engine failure	122.466
Takagi	Arrows	43	Gearbox failure	120.398
Badoer	Minardi-Ford	43	Engine failure	119.650
Coulthard	McLaren-Mercedes	39	Hydraulics/gearbox failure	122.995
Gené	Minardi-Ford	31	Gearbox failure	121.972
Hill	Jordan-Mugen-Honda	21	Withdrew	120.580
Panis	Prost-Peugeot	19	Gearbox failure	122.653
Trulli	Prost-Peugeot	3	Electrical failure	120.587
Zanardi	Williams-Supertec	0	Electrical failure	—

P I T - S T O P S

Lap		Duration* (sec)	Lap		Duration* (sec)
15	Wurz	33.147	31	Frentzen	30.362
15	Hill	39.703	31	Gené	39.882
16	Panis	31.053	32	Irvine	29.796
16	Gené	31.469	32	R. Schumacher	32.150
16	Fisichella	31.821	32	Badoer	37.510
17	Herbert	33.574	33	Barrichello	32.731
17	Villeneuve	32.563	33	Wurz	33.148
17	De la Rosa	39.950	33	Zonta	32.300
18	Badoer	32.320	33	Fisichella	32.136
19	Hakkinen	32.520	34	Coulthard	42.726
19	Frentzen	30.741	34	Villeneuve	32.514
19	Alesi	33.320	34	De la Rosa	35.848
19	Zonta	32.729	35	Takagi	34.668
19	Takagi	35.944	36	Herbert	36.468
20	R. Schumacher	31.046	36	Alesi	32.166
20	Barrichello	31.230	37	M. Schumacher	30.717
20	Diniz	32.294	38	Hakkinen	30.966
22	M. Schumacher**	29.771	37	Diniz	31.293
22	Coulthard	31.042	41	Badoer	38.561
23	Irvine	30.742			

*Including driving to and from pit . . . .** Fastest pit-stop

F 1   R A C E   C A L E N D A R   F O R   2 0 0 0

Australian Grand Prix	Melbourne	12 March
Brazilian Grand Prix	São Paulo	26 March
San Marino Grand Prix	Imola	9 April
British Grand Prix	Silverstone	23 April
Spanish Grand Prix	Barcelona	7 May
European Grand Prix	Nürburgring	21 May
Monaco Grand Prix	Monte Carlo	4 June
Canadian Grand Prix	Montreal	18 June
French Grand Prix	Magny-Cours	2 July
Austrian Grand Prix	A1-Ring	16 July
German Grand Prix	Hockenheim	30 July
Hungarian Grand Prix	Hungaroring	13 August
Belgian Grand Prix	Spa-Francorchamps	27 August
Italian Grand Prix	Monza	10 September
United States Grand Prix	Indianapolis	24 September
Japanese Grand Prix	Suzuka	8 October
Malaysian Grand Prix	Sepang	22 October

PICTURE ACKNOWLEDGMENTS

Picture research by Jo Walton and Will Hoon

All pictures by ALLSPORT/Chris Cole, Michael Cooper, Jonathan Ferrey, Mike Hewitt, Vincent Laforet, Jean Marc Loubat, Clive Mason, Pascal Rondeau, Mark Thompson, Vandystadt and Anton Want, Martin Whittaker, except the following:

Page 36, centre right: Rex Features/Denzil McNeeland
Page 65, top: Press Association/EPA
Page 85, top right: Sporting Pictures
Page 96, top left: LAT

DISCLAIMER
Every effort has been made to ensure that the details given in this book are accurate at the time of going to press. Neither the editor nor the publisher can accept any responsibility for any errors that may have occurred.

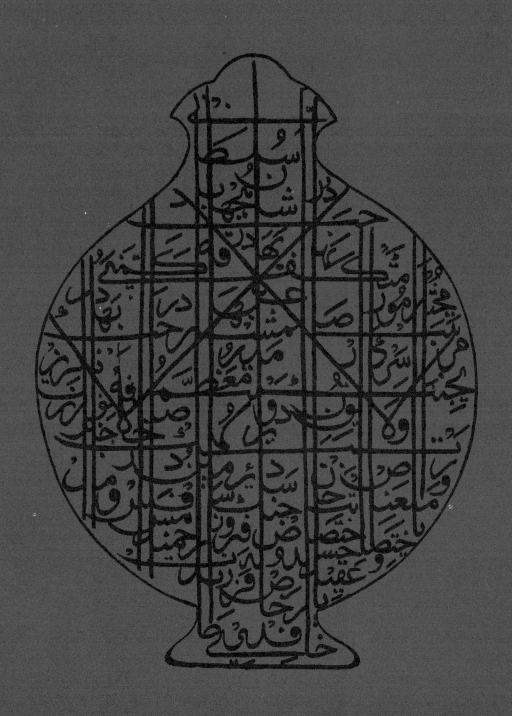